Praise for B2B Is Really P2P

This is the best book on selling that I've ever read. I want to stop right there and just say, "Any questions?" Frank Somma is a completely engaging and entertaining writer who delivers incredible value. He gets to the heart of what selling really is and then gets into the nitty-gritty of how to do it. If you are in sales or even remotely thinking about getting into sales, you have to read this book! — Joe Calloway, author, *The Leadership Mindset*

Frank Somma shares his life stories in such a humble way, that it allows us all to learn how to be a great person, not just a great salesperson. Frank has been my mentor for many years, and I know he can help you as well. I found *B2B Is Really P2P* to be a great roadmap in elevating our interpersonal skills.
— Peter Chieco, Certified Investment Management Analyst®

Frank Somma will inspire you, make you think, motivate you to take action and provide you with real world tools that work. Why? Because I've known Frank for over 30 years and he lives and breathes the art of successful selling every day! — Barry Farber, TV/Radio Personality, Entrepreneur and Co-Inventor of the FoldzFlat® Pen

Frank Somma crams more wisdom, experience and common sense into 200 pages than you find in books twice this size. Young people can certainly, benefit from what Frank shares, but there is plenty here for more experienced women and men, as well. — Lyle B. Dennis, Managing Partner, Cavarocchi-Ruscio-Dennis Associates, LLC

Not only has this book reignited some great skills I used in the past, especially when I was a newbie, but I have never been as proud to call myself a salesperson as I am right now. Thank you for providing profound life lessons, real sales techniques and strategies and, above all, the spark that's inspired millions of salespeople all over the world – a spark that has fueled my passion and hard work – all in a New York tone of purpose and drive.

I really expected to read something so different, but wow, you remind me of Napoleon Hill! Great storytelling, easy read, *I loved it!*
— Debbie Kosta, Live Event Sales for Tony Robbins, New York City

This book is so frank and also so "Frank" – his journey in sales and how he can help you in yours. Insightful, funny, honest and so true. Definitely a resource to re-read whenever you find yourself "falling off the tracks" in your ongoing sales approach. Frank gives practical advice to both the beginner and long-term salesperson, all with a focus on building strong relationships. A must-read for anyone in a sales capacity, which is almost everyone!

— Tom De Filippe, Managing Director, National Valuation Firm

You may think you've heard it all in sales, but you haven't heard it the Frank Somma way! Frank has a style that will inspire the reader to up their game. *B2B Is Really P2P*'s solid tools will arm the reader with the knowledge they need to catapult their business. I highly recommend this book for anyone who wants to boost their sales!

— Jane Atkinson, Speaker Launcher, author, *The Wealthy Speaker 2.0*

The honest truth? This is the best sales book ever written! Frank Somma is a genius storyteller. I'll be using Frank's quotes, stories and techniques for the rest of my career. — Dr. Rob Gilbert, Professor of Sport Psychology, Montclair State University

Frank's Italian heritage provides a colorful backdrop as he portrays today's fast-changing rules to acquiring customers. He looks at how sales professionals have learned to adapt and navigate these changing times to be successful while never forgetting the core qualities and traits that made them successful. Frank has hit a home run with *B2B Is Really P2P* and I recommend it to all sales professionals.

— Larry Weiss, CEO & President of Atlantic, Tomorrow's Office

I have had the pleasure of knowing Frank both professionally and through his extensive charitable work for decades and can honestly say that *B2B Is Really P2P* captures the essence of what is required to succeed in both worlds. It is written in layman's terms and is a roadmap for success. As clearly stated there are no shortcuts to success; however, I truly believe anyone willing to implement the principals and commitment to succeed as outlined in this book will reap tremendous benefits.

— Frank Fusaro, co-founder and President of The Forum Group

B2B

BUSINESS

BUSINESS

is really

P2P

PERSON

PERSON

 HOW TO **WIN** WITH **HIGH TOUCH** IN A HIGH TECH WORLD

Anyone Can Create Instant Rapport,
Build Strong Relationships and
Cement Long Term Loyalty

FRANK**SOMMA**

Copyright © 2019 by Frank Somma

ISBN: 978-0-578-61433-5

Edited by: Catherine Leek of Green Onion Publishing
Interior Design and Layout by: Kim Monteforte
Front Cover Design by: Brian Wrensen of Captain Creates

I dedicate this book to *"The Nine of Us." "The Nine of Us"* is my purpose in life. Every move, every decision, every thought and plan is made with *"The Nine of Us"* in mind. Each day I awake with overwhelming gratitude because we are *"The Nine of Us"* and because of what that intrinsically means to me. *"The Nine of Us"* is an ever-flowing river of joy and contentedness for me.

Vi Voglio troppo bene. Noi Nove = La Vita

Acknowledgements and Big Gratitude

I am most grateful to my mom Roseann who instilled a love of reading in me at a very young age and always had the utmost confidence in me. One of my earliest childhood memories is of her reading to my brother and sister and me. I vividly recall, with a deep feeling of warmth, leaning against her, my thumb in my mouth and my drowsy eyes moving from the unintelligible pages to her lovely face as she read from an ancient, tattered hardcover, *Black Beauty*. I was hooked! No pictures, just lots of pages and words that Mama made come alive! I couldn't wait until I could learn to read them like she did.

A few years later, in the second grade, I came home with a terrible end of year report card. This was in the sixties when our New York City school classes were divided into three distinct levels determined by standardized testing, the prior year's grades, and, I'm sure, some bias. Mom saw that report card and, with an unreasonable show of faith in me said, "You're obviously bored in this class. I will go to the principal and have her put you in with the higher group so you'll be properly challenged." And she did.

To my Dad from whom I learned some of my selling skills, lots of my negotiating skills, and most of my work ethic and discipline.

My older brother Al blazed an incredible trail to follow in books and music and shaped my tastes with his choices. He turned me on to Salinger, Roth, Proulx, Ford, and countless other giants of writing.

I'm grateful to my coach, the great Jane Atkinson who can deliver a correction like a too long, too tight hug from one of my old Italian aunts. As it begins, I'm not sure I want it at all but as it continues, I realize the warmth and caring behind it and how much I needed it. Whatever success I find as a speaker I owe to the knowledgeable, and patient guidance of the brilliant Jane Atkinson.

To each of my experts, Debbie Kosta, Frank Fusaro, Larry Weiss, and Peter Chieco. Thank you for sharing your time and wisdom so generously with me and with whomever reads this book.

To Brian Wrensen of Captain Creates, each design you do for me seems to hit the mark as you're able to graphically create what I can barely articulate. You've got mad talent!

Big love to my great friends Mike Sadoski and Bobby Kossin who read early versions of the book and came back with great suggestions.

To my mastermind partner, and longtime friend Jim Coler who helped me think through the process from inception to conclusion as he has done with every aspect of my business life for the past 30 years offering wisdom, insight, and most of all friendship and encouragement.

To Dr. Rob Gilbert who is so generous with his vast collection of anecdotes, poems, and sayings; he makes Santa look like a cheapskate. I do what I do because you told me I could, told me how to get started, and continue to give me advice and tips to make me get better.

To my editor Catherine Leek who is fiercely smart, patient, and kind and managed to keep track of everything while I kept track of nothing and never once made me feel like I was a burden.

To Kim Monteforte for being flexible and creating the perfect interior design.

To each of you who've offered superlative endorsements after reading the proof. I seriously cannot believe you liked my work that much. It is totally mind-blowing.

And, of course, to my darling bride who said "go for it" and stood with me, when at 59 years of age, I said I was going to quit my job, take a huge hit in the wallet, write a book, and build a speaking business. I promise I won't let you down. ILY

Contents

Selling to the Sopranos

The year was 2008. The mortgage market was in meltdown, banks were being bailed out by the Fed and sales, for us, had flat lined.

I was the newly minted national sales director for a large New York City cinema equipment reseller. Essentially, we sold the gear folks bought or rented to make the movies and television shows we all love to watch. Because most people making a movie or TV show rent, rather than purchase, we also had a rental company and served both markets – sales and rental. Great idea, right? Maybe not.

We were approaching the final quarter of 2008, our numbers were down, and we needed a strong quarter to hit our goal for the year. I was examining every aspect of our business, scrutinizing every proposal and looking under every rock when I went to my number one sales guy, Steve, to figure out what he could bring in for year-end. The meeting included a review of our largest potential opportunities and strategies to close them now, despite the sagging economy. The largest of those opportunities was a family-owned rental company in our own backyard, midtown Manhattan. It was owned and operated by two larger-than-life brothers – the Limans.

The Liman brothers were, as I said, larger than life, both figuratively and literally. They were real NY characters. Either of them could have stood on the justice scale, opposite Tony Soprano, and the scale would have stayed dead even.

Not only were the Liman boys physically large, but they lived large too. They both drove Rolls Royces, wore diamond studded

Rolexes on their sapling-sized wrists and were legendary for flying first class to our annual trade show in Vegas, renting a huge suite and sitting at the tables with big stacks of black chips in front of them and big crowds gathered behind them.

Looking at the account record, I called my sales guy out because we had done absolutely no business with them over the prior 9 months.

"What's with Liman Video Rental?" I chided. "These guys have to spend over a million dollars a year in cameras and lenses just to stay current but they haven't even bought a tripod from you. *Why not!?*"

Steve looked at me as though I'd just fallen to the earth (which, in this business, I had) and said, "They won't buy from us. We are their competition in rental and they said *they won't buy from their competitor*. A lot of the other rental companies feel that way too."

The pressure of the slumping sales and his matter-of-fact attitude about this were too much for me. I exploded. "*What do you mean they won't buy from us? Did they sit with ME? Did they tell ME they won't buy from us?* When we've exhausted all avenues, including a meeting with me, then you can say they won't buy from us. Until then, I don't want to hear that. You call those two mooks and tell them there's a new sheriff in town and he wants a meeting."

So he did. He set up a lunch at their favorite Italian restaurant in Hell's Kitchen.

It was a little hole-in-the-wall place, all the way over on 9th Avenue, surrounded by bodegas, coffee carts and raggedy people wheeling their life's possessions around in stolen shopping carts. I was surprised they hadn't picked Smith and Wolensky's or Morton's. From what I heard about these guys a fancy steakhouse seemed more their style.

When I entered the foyer to wait for them the first thing that hit me was the old school décor. When's the last time you saw red velvet wallpaper? The next thing that hit me was the smell. This place was the real deal. It smelled like my Grandma's kitchen on Sunday afternoon. I was ready to lay odds that there would be a crucifix on the wall and plastic covering the furniture.

As I waited for the Limans to arrive I was, to say the least, a nervous wreck. Here I was the new boss who knew nothing of the marketplace or this client and I had just thrown down a challenge to my best rep, claiming that I could be effective where no one before me had been. The scuttlebutt around the sales department was rife with talks about my naïveté and the beating I would take in this meeting with the infamous Limans. It probably sounded a lot like the chatter in David's camp the night before he met Goliath.

When they came through the door the owner of the restaurant treated them like they were Sinatra and Martin. He gave them a big hug, reaching almost a quarter of the way around them. "Boys! I'm so glad you're here! I have your favorite table set and I put out some of that special *prosciutto* and *parmigiano* that you love!"

For those of you who don't know, good prosciutto goes for about $35 per pound. Great prosciutto, aged for 2 years or so, can go for $100 per pound and that's before the restaurant marks it up. There was at least a pound of "the good stuff" mounded on the table along with as much parmesan as you're likely to see anywhere outside of Parma, Italy.

We sat and after some initial – introductions I went with my number one, tried and true, instant rapport builder – unabashed flattery.

"Thanks so much for coming out. I have heard about you for a long time now and it sounds like you built an awesome company. What do think the key to your success has been? How have you managed to build such a powerful business?"

The younger, and larger, of the brothers literally turned his back to me, looked at his brother and said, *"Do you believe this freakin' guy? He thinks I'm gonna tell him how to build his rental company."*

Then he turned back to me and said, "You're my competitor, you think I'm gonna tell *YOU* how to build a freakin' rental business? Get the eff outta here." Then they both shook with laughter and piled some more prosciutto on their plates.

> **"Do you believe this freakin' guy?
> He thinks I'm gonna tell him how
> to build his rental company."**

So much for my number one, tried and true, instant rapport builder.

Those were literally the first words spoken at lunch. I thought I was going to die. The look my sales guy gave me was a cross between smug and horrified if you can imagine such a look.

"Check please! We're done here" was on the tip of my tongue. But, then, we did have all that good prosciutto and cheese in front of us and I was going to have to pay for it anyway, so I made my own plate and went to the well to pull out all of the rapport training and communication skills I had studied and practiced for the past 20 years. I restarted with some benign, open-ended questions and stayed in "uptime",[1] totally focused on them.

I tuned in to every nuance of communication in an attempt to get off the mat after that first round knockout. I matched my body posture to whichever one was answering. I was hyper-aware of everything from their foot alignment to their breathing, hand positions, small nuances in the color of his complexion and the most fleeting micro expressions. I paid attention to the pace and tone of their voices and the preference in their predicate language choices. I did it all seamlessly and naturally lest I get called out as a mimic, an actor or, worse, *a salesman*!

At a glacial pace, I watched those massive shoulders begin to relax, those inner canthus re-emerge and those $800 Italian loafers begin to turn more toward the center of the table. I saw less cheek color, slower, lower breathing and the lines in the forehead and eyes begin soften. I kept at the questions, taking my turn to talk and involving Steve so this didn't feel like an interrogation. But the focus remained on sincerely learning all I could about these two men. If there was a chess clock on the table that each of us hit to time the duration of our speaking, at the end of hour one it would have been Frank and Steve 8 minutes and the Limans 52.

As the lunch wore on, they ordered grilled *pulpo*, fried calamari, *zuppa di pesce*, pasta with shaved truffles and tomahawk veal chops that looked like they should be on a *Flintstones* episode. They began to talk about the famous people they'd met, the movies and television shows they'd supplied cameras to and the sets they'd visited. They had great stories of celebrities and on-set shenanigans. They talked about the tricked out location van they were building to cover live events, their expensive cars, their huge homes and their big-ticket toys.

Fighting off a food coma, I continued asking open-ended questions with genuine interest and managed to find common ground in how we grew up, people and restaurants we knew from old NY, our love of the Yankees, hatred of Sox and where we were and who we'd lost on 9/11. After two-and-a-half hours, despite the rocky start, I was looking at two relaxed guys with real smiles that reached their eyes. I knew we were in rapport.

In fact, we gained enough rapport that, in the end, I was able to attack the dragon straight on and cut off his head. That's my overly dramatic way of talking about handling the original objection. I squared up and asked about their concerns with buying from us because we also had a rental company and were their "competition." I heard them out and, because we were definitely in sync now, I was able to offer an assurance about our rental business and how we were too small to compete with them and, for the most part, didn't even bid of the same jobs they did *and they trusted my word*. When we parted company, the dominant brother looked at Steve, my sales guy, and said, "Call me at the end of the week. I'll have a nice order for you."

The bill for lunch was over $500. But that was okay because before that Amex bill hit my mailbox, I had secured them a million dollar line of credit with our leasing partner and over the next 12 months they used every dime of it with us and applied for more.

We went on to develop a good business friendship. I genuinely liked them both. The year after that infamous lunch, I was invited to a fifth birthday party for the younger brother's daughter and the older brother invited me to his Long Island gun club to shoot trap and skeet with him.

Two years, and many lunches, dinners, and large sales later, the Liman brothers decided to split up and go their separate ways. The younger brother called me to ask if I would represent him to sell his half of the business.

We'd gone from "You're my competitor, you think I'm gonna tell YOU how to build a freakin' rental business?" to "I want you to represent me in the biggest transaction of my life." That is what understanding rapport does. That is what building a strong relationship will bring. That is the essence of who we want to become for our clients.

In the pages that follow I will lay out all I know about the science of communication and selling from a position of rapport. My expertise in selling this way comes from over 40 years of sales and sales management combined with over 40 years of studying. I am a certified practitioner of NLP (neuro-linguistic programming, the same communications science that vaulted Tony Robbins to the top of the motivational speakers' game). I have also read voraciously on sales and communications and have curated the best of what I've learned over the years. I've given hundreds of talks, written two books, lots of articles and almost 900 blog posts.

What you will find in the pages that follow are instructions on how you can quickly and easily gain rapport with almost anyone and build relationships and cement long-term loyalty. Selling is no longer "the art of the deal." It is now the art of the relationship.

In an Amazonian world where one can practically point and click to buy a luxury yacht, the role of the salesperson is drastically changed. It used to be that buyers relied on us to bring them information in order to make a buying decision. Now buyers likely know as much about what we're selling as we do and, in many cases, know a lot about us and our company as well.

If we are to be relevant in this new paradigm, what do we bring? Google has information gathering covered and the various websites, rating agencies and algorithms can provide customers with comparisons, pricing, ratings and FAQs. So where is our place? Why are we still essential?

> **If we, as salespeople, are to be relevant in this new paradigm, what do we bring? Where is our place? Why are we still essential?**

Our place is to shepherd our clients through the process; to help them learn the nuances that one cannot glean from looking at a 4.5 star rating. Our job is to find the buyers, the users of our products and services, and introduce them to the differences we bring versus services they may be using now. Our job is to position ourselves to be invited to the table and to be trusted and relied upon to not let that buyer look bad. Our job is to usher them through the process and mitigate the risk that comes along with contracting any new service. Our job is to look for pain and assuage it. Our job is to remain in touch and be welcomed into that customer's office long after the initial sale is made; to monitor and make sure we exceed the promises we made at the time of the sale. Our job is to be the conduit to our company and service and constantly ensure a good experience and to face, head on, any issues that could derail that good experience. Our job is to find the buyers, make them comfortable to buy, build on that relationship and create long-term loyalty.

That is what selling is today and to get there you've got to be well liked and well thought of. *B2B Is Really P2P* will give you the inside scoop on how the very best in the business do this. I've interviewed some of the most successful salespeople and entrepreneurs in the country from several different businesses so you can hear firsthand their take on high achieving sales today. In this book you will learn to break down human interactions to a granular level so that you can build rapport like you'd build a bridge across a wide span, connecting each side solidly rather than attempting to cross treacherous waters on a flimsy zip line, constantly worrying about collapse and the next gust of wind.

CHAPTER 1

Sales Is Not a Dirty Word!

I met an acquaintance for breakfast the other day. His name is Mark Curcio. He's an accountant.

When I mention that he's an accountant do you think sales? Not a chance! I mean, we call them "bean counters," right? The image that comes to mind for most of us is a nearsighted nerd bent over his ledger wielding a mechanical pencil complaining about one entry or another being categorized incorrectly. I figured the guy I was sitting across from at breakfast would reinforce, at least some of, my preconceived notions. But I couldn't have been more wrong. The stereotype I had in my head was not Mark.

As we spoke about our businesses, he surprised me by talking about the business development and the sales techniques he brings to bear in order to increase his revenue. He didn't say business development and sales techniques. I did. He spoke of how he works from home a few times a month and, when he does, he prospects. He did not use the word "prospect," but that's what I'm calling it.

Here is what Mark said.

> When I work from home I decide on a range of calls. Maybe it's the letters L to P today. I hit the contacts icon

on my phone; go to the first contact at letter L and call. I then call every contact in order until I get through the Ps. *If* I get through the Ps! It's a lot of calls. And even longer conversations. Four or five letters usually takes an entire day. I am not calling them for business. I am calling to catch up. Nothing more. I'm just a friend touching base.

Invariably these calls result in business. By the next day three or four of these people call back with projects requiring my help or, even better, a referral to someone they think could use my help.

Becoming the Blue Subaru

What Mark is doing is positioning himself for *selective attention*. Selective attention is all about awareness.

If I decide to buy a blue Subaru because I usually see green Subarus while driving around and I want to be different, guess what? As soon as I make the decision, there will be a virtual parade of blue Subarus presented to me as I go through my day. It's not that they weren't out here before, it's that I wasn't looking for them. It's like that in sales and that is precisely what Mark is doing.

When Leo Limoncello in Mark's contact list hears about a tax problem from a business associate, Leo may or may not call Mark, depending on his level of comfort in offering a recommendation, how many accounting professionals he knows and if Mark even enters his mind at that moment. But if he has recently spoken to Mark, Mark becomes the blue Subaru.

Mark has a very successful accounting practice in Manhattan and I am not surprised. Every successful business, at its core, is a sales company. Some other accountant may be able to memorize the new tax laws or do the square root of 3,364 in his head, but unless he goes out and finds people who want to hire him (*sells!*), his skills won't mean beans.

Selling Is a Skill

Selling skills are nothing more than a set of tools that will help to set you apart from the crowd. People with selling skills build rapport more quickly and sustain relationships longer. Well-honed selling skills can help you to be well respected, well thought of, well liked, well considered and well-remembered. These skills get folks to want to do favors for you and get you preferential treatment and discounts. They can be brought to bear to bring people around to your point of view or to help to ease tensions in inflammatory situations.

My accountant is awesome with numbers. He is very well trained and handles my tax problems with a deftness that keeps me from ever having IRS issues. My doctor has a degree from a prestigious medical school and has spent countless hours learning the science of the human body. She can easily diagnose my symptoms and offer relief from what ails me. But if the three of us go to a hockey game and want to move down closer to the ice, who do you think goes to speak to the usher? Me. The guy with the sales skills. I can't relieve pain and I don't know a debit from a credit. I can, however, convince an usher that he, and the franchise, would be better off with the three of us filling empty seats closer to the ice.

Your ability to relate, persuade and communicate will do more for your bank balance, personal relationships and overall career than any other set of skills you can master and that means sales skills.

Your ability to relate, persuade and communicate will do more for your bank balance, personal relationships and overall career than any other set of skills you can master and that means sales skills.

Sales has gotten a bad rap in our society. At the mention of sales skills people conjure up images of Danny DeVito in *Tin Men* or the famous ABC (always be closing) scene from *Glengarry Glen Ross*. The truth is we are all selling.

Peter Chieco, recognized as one of *The Financial Times* Top 400 Financial Advisors, had this to say when I asked him if he actually described himself as being in sales.

EXPERT TAKES

Yes. Although I don't market myself as a salesman, I clearly say it to the people in my business, especially the rookies. We are salespeople. It's not a bad thing; it's a good thing.

People have a bad perception of sales – like a used car pushy guy doing whatever he needs to do to close. It's true that if I don't sell I don't survive; it's a commission business. But we aren't about selling to hit quota. We are about serving our clients' needs at a very high level and to do that well you have to be good at selling.

We Are All Salespeople

The veterinarian sells you on heartworm pills for your dog. Moms and Dads are selling their kids on the importance of reading and the lawyer is selling the jury on the innocence of his client.

Who has a better chance to gain the favor of a fair maiden? The guy with no eye contact, half turned away, searching for the right words or the guy who is squared up, with soft eyes, asking questions and listening with respect?

At its very essence, this is where selling begins – bringing to bear rapport skills that allow other folks to be comfortable and open around you. Comfort and openness facilitate good communication and chart the path to the exchange and acceptance of ideas.

This is also where selling gets a bad rap. False flattering, flim-flam men laying it on thickly to gain inauthentic rapport in order to move people to a place for their own gain and the other person's loss is not selling; it's a crime! It's swindling, a scam, a cheat, a rook, a fleece. That person is a con artist, a swindler, a snake oil salesman ... wait! Snake oil salesman? ... Salesman? I see the issue.

You see, selling in my world, a world of professionals, isn't about deception. It's the opposite of deception. It is using a very specialized set of skills to get from point A to point B for the betterment of all parties involved. Selling, in my world, is helping. It's helping people to get unstuck, make choices, move forward or just feel better about where they are.

The Sales Gene

Let me tell you another story about that same accountant, Mark, with whom I shared that great breakfast. We were talking about meeting people and networking for business and he shared with me this awesome networking story.

Mark was invited to an event that took place during the first week of April. That's right, some bonehead created an event and expected an accountant to show up during the absolute busiest week of the year for accounting professionals.

As it turns out, the inviter worked for a large bank and the accountant, Mark, had a strong affiliation with that bank. Add to that, the inviter was the new rep from the bank and called to ask Mark especially to stop by. The event was at Madison Square Garden and Mark's office is close by. When the bank rep called Mark could hear the near hysteria in his voice, "It's a bust! Very few people are coming. Can you squeeze out an hour and at least stop by? I really need to pull this out of the ashes."

Mark, as I said, is an accountant. But he is a different sort of accountant. Mark has the sales gene. He is keenly interested in business development. He understands that being good at what you do will certainly get you some business but that, more importantly, people do business with people they know, like and trust and Mark makes it a point to get to know more people.

The sequestered April accountant is almost proverb but Mark broke the mold. The combination of the misguided organizer's need and Mark's commitment to business development won out and he decided to stop by the event for an hour. Around the cheese ball, as it were, he met one of the only other attendees. They made small talk about their respective businesses and in the course of that conversation Mark asked a simple question. "What is your greatest challenge right now?"

The guy went on to talk about a big problem he was having with security. He was in the wholesale distribution business and felt as though product was leaving out of the back door. His business had grown quickly and he did not have a very firm handle on inventory. I don't know the particulars but after that conversation, the guy hired Mark to help with his inventory situation. According to Mark, 5 years later, this guy is his firm's largest client.

Selling is not limited to those of us who make commissions to move a product or service for our company. Selling is the company. Whatever product or service you offer, you must offer. And those who tender it more frequently and with conscious selling skills will garner the lion's share of the business.

Today's Salesperson

I hate the stereotyping of salespeople. Think of it like ethnic stereotyping. Is it fair? Can we paint an entire group of people with one brush because they share a particular ancestry, religion, skin tone or preference? The other part of stereotyping that bothers me is that it is almost always negative and this is especially true in the stereotyping for salespeople.

I've known and respected the great Frank Fusaro for years.

A CPA, co-founder and President of The Forum Group, a 100-person, veteran-owned recruitment and consulting firm, lecturer on recruitment and retention, and philanthropist extraordinaire, so I refer to him as the great Frank Fusaro. Check out what Frank said when I asked him if he considered himself a salesperson.

EXPERT TAKES

Yes. A salesperson is not the first one with a lampshade on his head slapping backs at a party, a salesperson is someone who has intelligence, and very distinct work ethic. When I talk to young people about selling in this business, I say, you know, when I was a kid, there was a comic strip, Joe Palooka.

He was a very handsome, blond-haired, blue-eyed monster in the comic strips and they made this character into a toy. He was there in his boxing trunks. He was three of four feet tall; basically a big upright balloon with a metal piece, like a ball or something, in the bottom so you'd hit the toy and it would fall down backward and bounce right back up. Yes, that's what a salesperson has to be. He has to be the guy to take the punch and come back.

There are tools and approaches that you need to understand to be a good salesperson. But most of it has got to do with what's inside of you. And that's what most people don't have. And that's why salespeople are so coveted because they have that thing inside them that keeps going and they are the people that make the business run. Without sales you have nothing.

You could have the best product in the world, the best price but if you don't know how to sell it, it's not going anywhere.

Listen, I loved the movie *Tommy Boy* as much as the next guy but to say that Chris Farley's performance of Tommy Boy was an accurate portrayal of a professional salesperson is like saying that

Joe Pesci, in *My Cousin Vinny*, was an accurate depiction of a criminal defense attorney.

I love sales. I love the science of it. I love the process. I love meeting people and learning about their businesses. I love hearing about how they got started or what their particular challenges are now. I love connecting with them on a personal level, listening and seeking common ground to stand on. I love connecting them with other people I know for services they've expressed a need for. I love to be depended on and trusted as a fellow business associate and a great resource with sound judgment. I like to bury the typical sales stereotype and any possible doubt about my sincerity a little deeper every time I come through with what I said I would.

In my interview with Debbie Kosta she told me about her love for people and her natural ability to listen and how she turned that love and ability into a successful selling career. Debbie, Personal Results Specialist, is a top producer on Tony Robbins' live events sales team.

EXPERT TAKES

I studied to be a writer. I hated salespeople or at least I hated to be sold to. I thought they're fake! When I went to Cypress some people approached me and offered me a job with Robbins because I could speak English.

I went to the venue and saw a poster for Tony's event. Then I heard salespeople talking to clients and they were talking to them like they were friends. They gave encouragement, and advice like they were friends. I was surprised because I had imaged salespeople selling, *but these people were having good conversations.* This is what I do in my life anyway, and since I love people, I gave it a try.

The sales reps in that room were all experienced people and I wasn't, so I was intimidated. But as I listened to them and began trying it myself, I got more comfortable. I love speaking to people about what they want in life and how they can do it. I studied Tony's tools and saw them as the missing piece for a lot of folks I spoke with. I also had a good instinct about people – when to call and when to leave them alone so I wouldn't come across as a pesky salesperson. I am a very good listener which helped me a lot. I advise talkative salespeople to put the phone on mute if they have to. I listen to what they are saying and, maybe more importantly, to what they're not saying.

I love all of this because that is who and what I am. I am a professional salesperson, a trusted resource, a problem solver. I'm a person you go to for a favor. I'm the one you reach out to when you need my service, but even more, I am the one you think of even when you need other services. I am a professional salesperson. I am seen as connected, networked, in touch, plugged in and resourceful.

> **I am a professional salesperson, a trusted resource, a problem solver. I do this by employing all that I have learned about connecting with people because at its base, the very root of selling is connecting.**

I've studied my craft. I have honed my skills. I am deft at taking someone from antagonist to adherent or converting a detractor into a defender. I do this by employing all that I have learned about connecting with people because at its base, the very root of selling is connecting.

President and Chief Executive Officer of Atlantic-Tomorrow's Office, Larry Weiss provided some insight on his early days in sales.

EXPERT TAKES

In my first year at Xerox I was number one out of 80 sales reps in the branch. I realized quickly that sales is a profession, while most people think of sales differently. There is a low barrier to entry for a sales position. It's not like you need a lot of schooling or a specialized degree to get in, but I look at sales as a profession not unlike being a doctor or a lawyer. I think it requires as much education as a doctor or a lawyer, although maybe a different kind.

I was fair at everything but never really great at anything so I always felt I was successful. Good enough was good enough. Then I found selling.

After my first year at Xerox I felt like a real success. I made $21,432 in 1974 when the average household income was about $10,000. (It was actually $13,093 according to multpl.com.) I was on top of the world!

Then the next year made $36,000. I papered my mother's wall with $100 bills. The average income was still about the same. I knew I had hit my stride. I knew I loved sales and copiers. The success pushed me to learn more and more about sales and leadership and I'm still a student of the game. Sales and leadership became my passion and still is today!

Frank Fusaro feels the same way about the profession of selling. He is a big believer in paying for performance and loves to see people in his company produce big and earn big. While I sat with him he had to take a call from a guy who was considering a sales position with Frank. The guy was a salaried employee at a big hospital conglomerate. When he finished the call he was visibly upset. Frank knew he could offer this guy a better life but the guy was too afraid to take the risk. When he hung up Frank described his frustration and disappointment to me.

EXPERT TAKES

Okay. So what do I do with that? Because that's a kid that's got three years in recruiting and reached out to me because I have a need in my HR placement world. But this kid, he doesn't want to be a salesman, he doesn't want to, you know, be under a quota or whatever. So I try to appeal to someone like that and explain that my people are top line producers and very valuable to me. I feel like saying, you're missing the boat, they don't give a damn about you. They're about the medicine. They're about the patients. They're about revenue generation, right? They're not about HR. He says, "I enjoy servicing that area and being a business partner."

That's such a line of nonsense – business partner. You're basically a caddy, and you're servicing the golfer, right? So you go to the golfer and say, "What do you need?" Okay, I'll try and find it. Right?

Conversely, if you came here, and you go out and recruit a guy for a hundred grand, you get a nice commission. Over there you get an attaboy from the company. When you find someone for double or triple that salary, which is not uncommon, you generate a five-figure commission for yourself. So what do you want? A five-figure commission or an attaboy from the hospital?

My Offer to You

My offer to you is to share with you the best of what I've learned over the past 40 years. I will do this by bringing to bear as many useful experiences as I can share and what I've learned from them. I've always been a student of the game. Whether it was my formal education in neuro-linguistic programming (NLP) or the one of the hundreds of sales, business, personal development and leadership books I've read or one of the many audio programs I own, podcasts I've listened to or seminars I've attended, I have curated the best of what I've found, tried most of it and can relate it to you here in stories or straight up techniques you may want to try. I've managed to find a usable gem, even in programs I thought missed the mark.

My hope here is that you'll be reminded of some things you learned before but may have forgotten or that I will prompt you to do some of the things that used to be in your arsenal but have since gotten rusty. I hope you'll relate to some of the stories and be able to equate the lessons in them with things you've done or things you're doing now. I hope to break some new ground and reveal some things you haven't considered before but will now be curious enough to try. While I do want to be somewhat thought provoking, my goal is to be action provoking. I want you to read these stories and lessons and grab the tools from them to use in your next sales or relationship encounter. I want you, through the application of these tools and techniques, to become a world-class communicator. Whether you're a seasoned sales veteran or sales leader or a Gen-Next college grad just starting out, I want you to read this and say "Ah, yes I see that. I want to be like that."

First and foremost we must accept that we are responsible for our results in life. We are but a choice away from changing it all if we desire.

> **First and foremost we must accept that we are responsible for our results in life. We are but a choice away from changing it all if we desire.**

We must accept that we are responsible for the results of our encounters and how we respond. That sounds obvious doesn't it, but you'd be surprised how often we blame others for not understanding us or making us unhappy. We even blame others for our responses with phrases like "You make me so angry" or "She made me yell about it." This isn't to say that provocation does not exist but, regardless of being baited, in the end, we choose our response. He doesn't make me angry. I choose anger in response to his incitement. It is within my power to choose understanding, mild disagreement or even apathy if I desire. To be successful we need to become accountable for our own state of affairs.

Recognizing and working on our own foibles regarding stimuli and response is a lifelong endeavor, however, once we begin the process we can begin to work on gaining rapport and building relationships. You can see how the two go hand in hand, can't you? How can you expect to gain rapport and build strong relationships if you're still prone to old programming and fly off the handle or recede into your own mind when old triggers present themselves?

This is all part of better communication and I will share many techniques that, once practiced and honed, become "the way you do things" and will replace some of the old, obsolete programming you've taken in over your life and will allow you to build long-lasting relationships in business and in life.

And while this will all serve you in every aspect of life, business is the main focus of *B2B Is Really P2P*. We will discuss how no one is truly a "natural" in sales. We'll talk about my belief that you don't lack talent, only technique. Having an aptitude or desire for selling is great, but developing some practices and systems will refine your proficiency and sharpen your expertise.

After using these techniques for many years, building many long-standing relationships in work and personally, I'm going to start with a personal story that had me flummoxed until I sought out some help.

PART ONE

PERSONAL RESPONSIBILITY

EXPERT TAKES

I asked Peter Chieco, a senior director at a major brokerage house with over $2 billion under their management, what three simple bits of advice he would offer a salesperson. Peter says:

1. Get in earlier than everyone else.
2. Ask the best advisors how they made it, take notes and review with them often.
3. Network like your life depends on it.

CHAPTER 2

Meet Them Where They Are

I have been a sales expert and motivational speaker for many years. My blog, "Weekly Thought," began in 2001 after the towers went down. It was my way of sending positive thoughts out at a time when fear and frustration were rampant and positivity was scarce.

The blog is a projection of my persona. I am an upbeat, you can do it, go get 'em, kind of guy. My voicemail greeting has always been some version of "Hi, it's Frank and I'm having a tremendous day! I hope you are as well. Leave a message and I look forward to speaking with you as soon as I possibly can."

My friends, family and coworkers have to endure this daily, even when they aren't in the best of moods. Throughout my life, even when I didn't feel like it, I put on my best face and did my utmost to remain upbeat and positive. This, I later learned, is not always appropriate or useful. To be clear, I didn't dance into funerals or fiddle as Rome burned but when I encountered someone in a bad way, I did my best to try to motivate them and bring them up. Then, my brother suffered a terrible accident.

I won't go into the details but at age 49 my extremely handsome and athletic brother had an accident that resulted in him becoming a quadriplegic. He went from riding his bicycle, adroitly weaving in and out of traffic — and pissing off cabbies — on the busy streets of Manhattan to having to be lifted in and out of bed with a hoist in an acute rehabilitation center in New Jersey. It was, to say the least, an enormous tragedy.

As his therapy progressed he was able to do some rudimentary things but he still relied on others to dress, feed and bathe him. I visited him often and we talked for hours. I often felt, though, that our time together was a bit inauthentic. I could see that my brother was "keeping a stiff upper lip," as they say, as he tried to deal with the devastatingly difficult life that was thrust upon him and I couldn't help but feel that he was doing that for me. I think he expected me to be all "You can do it, bro. You will overcome this, rah rah rah!" and he did his best to hide any depression from me. I could sense that I was doing him a disservice and wanted to be there for him in a more meaningful way.

Calling on the Experts

Seeking answers, I went to visit a good friend of mine, Dr. Dan Shaeffer, who has a Ph.D. in bereavement psychology and is NLP (neuro-linguistic programming) educated as well. I explained to Dan that I felt as though Al and I were just surface skimming and not really connecting. Dan taught me a great lesson. He said, "Meet him where he is." Dan taught me that you cannot move anyone anywhere until you first meet them where they are.

I was trying to cheer my brother up, he was trying to show me a good face and all the while, he was depressed and I was feeling like a lousy brother and friend. When Dan taught me this very important concept I was like, "Duh, of course!"

Essentially, you don't push, you lead. This applies in every aspect of communication and is essential in building trust and rapport. *Meet them where they are.* If a person is troubled, you must first understand the trouble and feel it from their perspective before you can

begin to think about helping them to solve it. And, more importantly, maybe you don't ever solve it. Maybe being a soft ear and
an empathizing party is all you're supposed to be.

> **Meet them where they are. You cannot
> move anyone anywhere until you
> first meet them where they are.**

The next time I visited my brother, after our initial greeting, I
looked him in the eye and said, "I can't imagine how bad this sucks
for you and how hard it is for you, all day, every day. I am so sorry
you have to live like this." My eyes welled up as I said it with all
of my heart because I felt every word. I had taken off my mask and
allowed myself to be who he needed me to be, and who I really
needed to be. Then, as though some magical portal had opened
between us, we cried together.

I thought I was supposed to bring him up. I thought I was supposed to be his strength. I thought I was supposed to *motivate him.*
All of that might have been true but none of it could happen until
I met him where *he* was, until I sat in his pain with him. Only then
could I begin, slowly, to try to help him see a brighter future – and,
again, the most important lesson here is that maybe I wasn't meant
to help him to see that brighter future. Maybe I was just to meet
him where he was and stay there with him, for him.

Where Are You Meeting Your Clients?

It is the same in selling. It's true that we are problem solvers but
you can't simply walk in with all the answers. People need to vent.
They need to describe the issue and feel as though you really get it.
They won't take a solution from someone who they feel doesn't
relate. Solutions like that feel like a whitewash, like a weak veneer

to cover up a crack rather than to repair it. It makes the salesperson look inauthentic and serves to fulfill the awful stereotype really good salespeople spend so much of their selling lives overcoming.

Let the popcorn stop popping!

I do some customer service training from time to time and share this phrase, "Let the popcorn stop popping!" It means that you need to allow the person to unpack the entire situation, even if you have a solution for them ready to go. I conducted one such training session at a home health care agency and one of the phone reps told this story.

> Mr. Jones wanted to switch the time his aid came in from the morning to the afternoon. This was a reasonable request and I have the authority to grant it if the schedule permits. I looked at the schedule and saw that his aid was, indeed, available for Tuesday and Thursday afternoons which were Mr. Jones' days.
>
> Almost as soon as he said, I'd like to switch to afternoons, I interrupted with. 'Okay, Mr. Jones, Molly is open. I will make the switch now and she will see you next Tuesday at 1PM.' Mr. Jones stumbled on his next few words, obviously thrown by my quick reply, and went on to tell me why he wanted to switch.
>
> It turned out, that after a bit of prompting by me, Mr. Jones was actually interested in a different home-aid worker but was uncomfortable saying such, so he went with a time change hoping that the afternoons were handled by another aid. Had I not recovered, drawn him out and listened, he might have called a different company and fired us entirely.

If you can relate to your clients' problems and empathize with their issues, you'll go a long way to building rapport. You will be leading them toward a solution that you've come to together, rather than pushing them toward a cookie-cutter answer. It's all on you.

Sometimes meeting your clients where they are can be quite difficult. As a financial advisor, Peter Chieco often has to speak with people when they are most vulnerable.

EXPERT TAKES

I'm very good at protecting families when there is a life event.

Sometimes, you have a strong leader who is heading the investment charge for the family and when he or she is gone, often, the remaining family members are at a loss of what to do. This is when we shine best and the plan we created previously allows for peace of mind.

I also try to help to guide the family leader to see a way for the family after he or she is gone so it is sustainable. We continually stay in touch with our clients, so we don't miss the opportunities to add value.

When I first started as national sales director for the cinema equipment company I mentioned in my opening story, I overheard some employees talking trash about a client in the hallway. I stuck my head out and asked them to come into my office and explain what they were talking about. It seems that the client they "couldn't stand talking to" was the owner of a small rental company not unlike us.

Companies, like ours, that rent cinema gear often sub-rent from one another at wholesale rates when we don't have a particular piece of gear to complete the package. According to the employees, every time this woman called to sub-rent from us, she made it clear that she was only doing this because she had to and that she'd rather sub-rent from anyone else but we were the only company that happened to have the piece of gear on hand that she needed in the moment. They said she was really bitchy and they all tried to pawn her calls off on to one another so that they wouldn't have to serve her. I asked what the source of her ire was and they said, "We don't know. She says that Rich (one of the owners of our company) did her wrong years ago."

I asked for her number and placed a call to her. I introduced myself as the new sales director and asked if we could talk. She was very closed and curt with me, answering my questions with one word answers or sarcastic remarks. She obviously felt wounded by us in some way but was not forthcoming with the origin of her insult. After a bit she began to elaborate and gave me an earful about how we thought we were a big company and didn't need business from a little shop like hers and how she avoided us whenever she could.

I asked to come by and visit the next morning and, I guess because I listened until the popcorn stopped popping, she said yes. I showed up with two hot lattes and a bag of Italian biscotti. (What can I say, I'm Italian. I was taught that when you visit, if you have a free hand to knock on the door, you haven't brought enough food and wine with you.)

We sat and chatted and it turned out that the perceived insult was over a lack of attention by our owner. She had an issue and had called and asked for him to resolve it. He delegated the resolution to the manager of the department, for which I really can't fault him. Unfortunately, besides not loving the resolution, she felt slighted by the delegation and proceeded to vilify Rich over it. The incident itself was small but, like with many people, she had magnified the insult over time. Each time she had to sub-rent from us she got angrier and added wood to the non-existent fire.

I listened for a long time and after the lattes, biscotti and the recitation of the entire story from her viewpoint, I was in enough rapport to be able to offer some other explanations that didn't depict

Rich as a bad guy. In fact, in the end, she conceded that in Rich's position she very possibly would have done the same thing.

I assure you that there is no way we could have gotten to a place of rapport strong enough to change her perception without allowing the popcorn to stop popping completely.

CHAPTER 3

It's All on You

It's on you. You are responsible for the results of your encounters.

It's on you. You are responsible for the results of your encounters.

Most people have a tough time swallowing this one. After a misunderstanding, most people would rather say, "she misunderstood me" or "that's not what I meant" or "they just don't get it."

All of those statements may be true at any given time and ... SO WHAT!?

Where Is that Smell Coming From?

I will never forget my first business trip to California. I was excited because the company was flying me out there and putting me up in a nice hotel and because I would get to see my uncle Conrad, who had moved out there with his family 20 years earlier.

My uncle, coming from NYC, constantly complained about the lack of good Italian delicacies in California and I was excited to go to his favorite *salumeria* in NY and fill a bag with Pecorino-Romano,

Coppocola, Mortadella and Sopressata. I must have bought 20 lbs. of great Italian cheeses and dried meats. I stuffed it all into my gym bag and carried it onto the plane to make sure it all arrived with me and didn't become "lost luggage," if you know what I mean.

The flight was smooth. I landed and grabbed a cab to my hotel in Laguna. I had the name and address of the hotel but it meant nothing to me until I arrived there. I had never stayed in a Ritz Carlton before. There are a lot of luxury hotels out there but, for me, Ritz Carlton stands alone. I was blown away. I walked into a beautiful lobby that led to a gorgeous bar and a restaurant with an outside terrace that opened to the Pacific Ocean. I sat out there with a glass of wine and thought "Wow, this is how rich people live."

I settled into my room, read a little and fell asleep quickly in that awesome, luxurious Ritz Carlton bed. I woke up early the next morning but my first meeting didn't start until 9 so I ran down the stairs to the gym super early to get a workout in and have plenty of time to grab breakfast on that beautiful terrace. It was early so I didn't expect to see anyone else but there was one guy on the elliptical machine.

As I settled myself onto the treadmill next to him, it hit me like a wet towel across the face; he smelled. The guy stunk! I'm not talking a little sweaty; it was a locker room funk type smell. I'm talking knock a buzzard off a roadkill type smelly. I decided cardio wasn't important and moved over to where the dumbbells were, but I could still smell him. I went to a further corner of the gym, but no luck; the place just wasn't big enough. I thought I'd have to alternate between holding my breath and breathing through my mouth for the remainder of the workout but, mercifully, he left about 5 minutes after I got there.

I attempted to breathe a sigh of relief but, guess what? The smell lingered. It was like the guy put a pall over the whole space. I couldn't escape it. I finally got through with my workout and headed for the elevator. When I got in and the doors closed, the smell hit me.

The guy had left a good 30 minutes before but his funk was so bad it remained in the elevator.

I thought about that for a minute. How could the smell be that pungent a half hour after the dude left? Just then a new thought occurred to me. I grabbed the front of my shirt and lifted it to my nose.

It was me! I stunk!

I had carried Uncle Conrad's cheeses in the bag with my gym clothes. The smell was coming from me the whole time!

As you read, this guy is probably at some meeting entertaining the group with his 100th recitation of the time he abandoned the elliptical, mid-workout, because some dude came in and stunk up the gym!

Anyway, the point is this, it's always easier to point to someone else. But before you say your boss stinks, or your job stinks or your coworkers, family, friends, or clients stink, you better check yourself first. You are responsible for the results of your encounters.

How Does Being Misunderstood Serve You?

You entered the encounter to make a point. Does being misunderstood serve you? Does identifying that you have been misunderstood serve you?

Perhaps it helps to assuage your feeling of failure when you relate it to someone else, emphasizing how right and sound and obviously misunderstood you were, but it's still a failure. Justifying it may help you feel a bit better in the moment, but what did it do for you really? Didn't you go into the encounter with a purpose and didn't you fail at that purpose because you were misunderstood? Wasn't success in the encounter what you really wanted?

This is why I say you are responsible for the results of your encounters – because you want to be. If you want to impress a point upon someone else and they misunderstand you, the end result is that you have not made your point. You have not done what you set out to do. Blaming the other person won't change that.

Making Your Point

What I propose is that you take this responsibility seriously and try a different route to make your point when you are misunderstood. If that doesn't work, try yet another route and take the responsibility of refashioning your point until you feel as though understanding has been gained.

To the unskilled this refashioning can come across as badgering or nagging. Wearing a person down until they yell "Uncle!" and give into your way isn't what I am talking about. Nor am I advocating an endless diatribe or twisting the same thing around ten different ways until you've exhausted yourself and your listener. I'm proposing you bring to bear the skills I will define in the pages that follow and increase dramatically the odds of being understood more quickly.

Beyond your interactions, I think you are responsible for just about *everything*.

Create Your Weather

Metaphorically, not meteorologically, I believe that I make the weather. I decide if it's sunny or cloudy. I create the rain, fuel the storms and sustain them with the intensity and duration of my choosing. I believe this strongly.

Debbie Kosta told me she doesn't hear the word "no."

EXPERT TAKES

I don't hear "no." I don't hear objections. I say a prayer that God will help me to help people.

I believe in what I do. I can't let go of someone who I believe needs this. That's why I don't hear "no." I envision them in the room.

I envision them having the life they want, that they've shared with me and I don't hear "no." I hear "not yet," so I don't let them go.

It helps that I don't chase after the money. A lot of people work triple what I work because they are focused on the wrong thing. I focus on the person and the money follows.

It is never about what happens to me but rather my reaction to what happens to me. How else would you explain this paradox? On one hand we have happy newlyweds with nothing but a cot and a table, in a cracker box of an apartment, laughing and eating peanut butter sandwiches while trying to manage bills with a negative bank balance. On the other hand we have a miserable multi-millionaire sitting alone in his ten-thousand square foot home, complaining that his taxes are too high, his gardener sucks and the grandchildren left the pool area a mess.

It's never about what I have and always about what I appreciate.

It's never about what I have and always about what I appreciate. That's the philosophy I choose to adopt. That's a philosophy I choose to feed daily with my gratitude journal lest I become callous, complacent or cynical.

I lose deals all the time. I power dial through dozens of unreturned sales calls each month. I have had doors slammed in my face – figuratively and literally. My roof has leaked, my power has gone out and my car has failed to start. I've been stuck in traffic, had flights cancelled and sat for hours at my local DMV. I've been yelled at, ignored, disrespected and disgraced. I've been fired, demoted, passed over and over worked. I've been fooled, lied to, set up and knocked down. I've experienced sickness, pain, injury and death. I have felt heartbreak, sadness and hopelessness. I have lived through whatever difficulties life has thrown at me to a greater degree than some and lesser degree than others.

My belief, my philosophy that I lead with gratitude and create my own weather stays in the forefront of my mind because I have chosen to mount it there, like a shield taking on all comers. I believe the world is just reflection of what I present to it and I choose to present myself with energy, thoughtfulness, consideration, gratitude and positive energy.

This great quote from George Bernard Shaw was one of the first to take a hold of me and help me to begin to shape a philosophy of my own.

> This is the true joy in life, the being used for a purpose recognized by yourself as a mighty one; ... the being a force of Nature instead of a feverish selfish little clot of ailments and grievances complaining that the world will not devote itself to making you happy.

I am a force of nature and, no, I never want to be a feverish selfish little clot of ailments and grievances. Like Shaw, I do not believe the world needs to devote itself to making me happy nor do I think it can make me happy. Happiness is an inside job.

CHAPTER 4

Your Actions and Reactions

It's human nature to blame others for where we find ourselves. But as we've been discussing we must be accountable, we must take personal responsibility – for our encounters, for our attitudes and philosophies, for our actions and reactions.

If you really think about it, playing "the blame game" makes no sense. The results we get will be ours to own and live with so why allow anyone else to shape those results? When we blame others, we are allowing them to fashion our results. By taking responsibility for our encounters we take ownership of the results. The good news is that when it's us, even if it goes badly, it's ours to refashion to a better outcome. If it's someone else's fault, what can we do but live with it?

Mastermind Check In

One of the best ways I keep myself in check is through my mastermind groups and coaching. I'm in two mastermind groups. One is more formal and has a facilitator. The group is a very safe place with like-minded individuals (we are all professional speakers), so we are able to share lots about our wins and losses and get unvarnished feedback from people who have been where we are now.

It's similar with my coach, the great Jane Atkinson. She and I speak once a month and I review my business plan with her. She holds me accountable for the things I haven't done and gives me praise for the things she sees me doing well. We talk about what some of her other clients are experiencing so I get to check myself against their experiences.

My other mastermind group is really a partnership. I meet often with Jim Coler, my friend and business associate (you will hear more about him later in the book). Jimmy and I are the same age and share similar philosophies of business but possess vastly different skill sets. We talk about one another's business ventures and opine with complete candor about what we like or dislike and agree or disagree with. We trust each other emphatically so it isn't possible for a suggestion or comment to come across as insulting or anything other than helpful.

I hope you have a Jimmy in your life or belong to a mastermind group. If not, at the very least I urge you to do two things.

1. **Find a coach.** Having someone with no horse in the race to talk about how you race your horse is incredibly valuable.

2. **Think about your business friendships.** Think about people you admire in business, people whose actions appeal to you as a businessperson. Then invite them out for a coffee. Begin the conversation about your businesses and philosophies and, maybe, over time you will find your Jimmy.

When I asked Larry Weiss about his mentors and role models he told me about two long-standing relationships. And, by the way, I've had scheduled breakfasts with Larry a few times a year for a couple of dozen years. He's been gracious with his time and has been a valuable mentor to me.

EXPERT TAKES

I've had many different people throughout my selling career and have learned from all. As far as a true mentor? My first trainer was not responsible to train me but he took me under his wing. He was a territory rep at Xerox, not a manager. I am still in touch with him.

I have a business coach and have worked with her for over 20 years and she is also my mentor.

The Defining Pause

Life is never about what happens to us but, rather, how we react to it. Let me ask you a question. Do you pull your sister's hair?

Seriously. If your sister pisses you off do you grab a handful and yank it like you were on Jerry Springer? Why not? You did this when you were two so why not now? Because between the time you were two years old and now you've learned some coping skills. What we see in the world is that some of us have learned a bit more than some others.

I believe the pause between thought and speech defines you. Some folks seem to have a greased chute from head to mouth. A thought occurs and out it comes with no inspection or governance; without a moment's pause to consider the effect. Regardless of the stimuli I believe the ultimate outcome is my responsibility.

It could be that I'm cocky but I am certain that when a bit of hostility or disrespect comes my way it is *my reaction*, not the hostility or disrespect that determines the outcome. I believe that I have developed a good number of tools over the years that allow me to select the proper one and shape the balance of the encounter to be more akin to what I want or at least to minimize the damage.

The tools and communications skills I am sharing in *B2B Is Really P2P* can become second nature so that the pause – that life-defining pause – becomes imperceptible. The ability to pause, think and react well becomes like moving the fork to my mouth to eat. I don't think, "Let me lift my hand and bend my elbow and steer these food laden tines toward my mouth." I just do it.

***

I believe the pause between thought and speech — that life-defining pause — defines you.

***

Unconscious Competence

Do you remember "the miracle on the Hudson?" In January 2009 Captain Chesley "Sully" Sullenberger landed an Airbus jumbo jet safely on the Hudson River.

The quote from Sully that I want to reference here drives home the point of mastery I referred to earlier – the ability to do something by rote because it is so ingrained in your subconscious from hundreds or thousands of hours practicing it. In an interview, Captain Sullenberger said:

> One way of looking at this is that for 42 years I've been making small, regular deposits in this bank of experience, education and training. And on January 15 the balance was sufficient so that I could make a very large withdrawal.

I read this as mastery. I read this as unconsciously competent (more on this concept in Chapter 11). It means that Captain Sullenberger trained hard and continued to grow through experience to the point that even a failed Airbus couldn't shake him from his practiced, ingrained moves and he was able to land that thing safely and save hundreds of lives.

This is the level of mastery I am looking for in communication. I want to be in a conversation, really in it. I want to listen actively and show the other person total attention and at the same time I want to calibrate masterfully. I want to see, hear and feel the emotions behind the words and this ability only comes from constant practice and focused learning.

The Big Wave

To finish up on personal responsibility and illustrate my belief that I am responsible for my environment and that I create the weather, let me tell you of a social experiment I have been conducting for about 15 years.

I was jogging in my neighborhood and had the sun at my back. As I made my way down the street I saw a car at the end of the block coming in my direction. It was a dark colored sedan like my friend and neighbor Bob drives and I thought, "I wonder if that's Bob Shirvanian?" As the car got closer, I strained to see who was driving but the sun glare was too strong and I could not see inside the car. I decided to smile and give a big wave in case it was Bob. As the car got closer and closer the glare receded, like a curtain being lifted from the windshield, and I could make out the total stranger waving back at me and smiling. I thought, "Hmm, that's interesting."

So as the next car got to about 25 yards out, I smiled and waved again. Again, as the glare receded I saw another stranger waving at me. For the next three cars I didn't wave and guess what? No one waved at me either. For the next four cars I waved and smiled and went four for four on return waves and smiles. I proceeded to do this for the duration of my run and it worked out the same each time. I wave, they wave; I don't, they don't.

I thought, maybe it's a Jersey thing so I tried it in New York. Same results. I tried it in Texas, California and in Washington DC.

Same results. I tried it overseas in Spain, London and Italy and got the same results.

The point is this. The world is nothing but a big mirror reflecting back to you the face you bring it every day.

The world is nothing but a big mirror reflecting back to you the face you bring it every day.

You see, I set the tone; I create the weather. Every day and, in fact, in every moment I have a choice and that choice is my attitude. I can't choose what happens to me but I do choose my reaction to it and for me that choice is a conscious, positive choice as often as I can muster it.

It's on you. You create the weather.

I will finish this section with a great Italian saying I have learned and adopted regarding people complaining about their problems.

"Chi causa del sua male piange lo stesso." Which loosely means, "People cause their own problems and then cry about them."

PART TWO

GAINING
RAPPORT

EXPERT TAKES

Larry Weiss says salespeople fail because of:

- Poor work ethic
- Laziness
- Poor attitude
- Lack of effort

CHAPTER 5

Learning to Communicate Better

I went to school for NLP – neuro-linguistic programming. It is a communication science developed by Richard Bandler and John Grinder that studies, at a micro level, how we humans communicate.

The Science of Communication

Bandler and Grinder spent a good portion of their lives decoding communication down to its very core elements.[2] They catalogued things like facial expressions, eye movements, breathing patterns, tone and pace of speech. They documented and recognized communication types by virtue of the words chosen and the way they were delivered. They called these *representational systems* and, while I will not attempt to run an NLP course in this book, I do wish to present to you my take on some of this learning and how I use it to improve myself and others in the professional world of selling.

Bandler and Grinder created what they called a "therapist training group." Their focus was to develop more effective therapists through the recognition, respect and use of these nuances of human communication, especially the relationship between word patterns, cues and behavior. Think of the power of that!

Understanding representational systems is like learning to speak Mandarin in time for your trip to China. These nuances of communication are the very language of the person you are speaking to. This is an enhancement. It is the language inside the language you both are speaking. Speaking in the same tongue does not mean you understand or are understood. We've all seen the after effects of wayward communication – bad feelings, lack of trust, suspicion.

As I previously mentioned, this science skyrocketed Tony Robbins into the aristocracy of motivational speakers. Tony was a student of NLP and used many of the techniques to help people get unstuck.

Putting the Science into Practice

As professional salespeople the very essence of what we do depends a lot on our ability to understand people and gain rapport. Some of us do this far better than others. You've no doubt heard of "women's intuition"? This wonderful ability to see beyond what is said or presented was often referred to as women's intuition whether the enlightened one was a man or a woman. What people were describing was an ability to listen, observe and subconsciously calculate the sum of what they heard, saw and felt in an effort to predict future behavior or to see past obvious behaviors that were not indicative of the problem but rather masking the problem.

Let me tell you a story about what prompted me to finally enroll in an NLP practitioner course and get certified in this great communication science.

My friend and business associate Jim Coler and I were walking into our office after a meeting outside. We were engaged in a conversation about the meeting as we passed through the door. The receptionist was sitting there and we both said "Hi Michelle."

Michelle said hello back and we walked up the stairs to our offices. Midway up the flight Jim looked at me and said, "Whoa, I have to remember to speak with Michelle later and find out what's wrong."

"What's wrong?" I said.

"Yeah, she obviously has something bad going on in her life." I scratched my head.

"And you know that because we said hello and she said hello back? Who are you, Kreskin?"

"Frank, didn't you *see her*? It was pouring out of her." I was seriously taken unawares. I looked back at our encounter in my mind's eye and didn't see anything that would indicate to me that Michelle was having trouble. I took the hello as just what it was, a hello, and moved on from there.

Stop when you say, "Hi." Stop and look at the person for a beat and calibrate.

As it turned out, Jim was, of course, correct. Michelle had a major family issue that was weighing heavily on her. What I learned is that Jim, and a select few others out there, are naturally tuned in. They have that women's intuition and pick up on the subtle clues that are there for any of us to see. Part of that came from "being where he was." In other words, I said hello in passing; Jimmy said hello and hung there for a beat. He was focused on the person and the greeting. He was mindful of what he was doing, not just shooting a greeting out because there was a warm body he had to pass by to get to his office. Learning to see what Jim saw – and beyond – became an obsession for me. I enrolled in NLP and have continued that line of study ever since.

Think for a moment about the power of this learning – the ability to tune in and gain rapport quickly and genuinely; the sense to know when to speak and when to back off; or the instinct to realize that someone is in peril and needs help even when they don't ask. Imagine having built in to your persona the increased likelihood of getting folks to see your point of view, push your project forward, sell your wares or endow your charity. Better communication enables better outcomes and better outcomes are what we all seek in every moment of every day.

CHAPTER 6

Rapport Feats and Foibles

So what are the keys to gaining rapport?

People do business with people they like and people do business with people they trust. To sell something – anything – you need to be liked or trusted, and understanding the skills you need to gain rapport will bring you both.

> **People do business with people they like and people do business with people they trust.**

Foibles

Before I tell you about the feats, let me first tell you the two most important rapport killers to avoid.

1. Trying too hard
2. Going too fast.

Trying Too Hard

Remember that kid in the schoolyard who really wanted to fit in with a particular group? Remember how hard he tried? What happened? He was rejected. It's a horrible cycle and it goes like this.

There is a group in place. A kid who isn't really a fit in that group wants to join in. He doesn't wait to be invited; he jumps right in. He's nervous. He knows he isn't really a fit so he tries extra hard. What happens then? The extra hard serves to magnify what a bad fit he is and he is rejected faster and harder. Next he steps up his effort to fit in, which, again, magnifies what a bad fit he is and again he is soundly rejected.

In his mind he can't comprehend what's happened. He has been taught his whole life that greater efforts produce greater results. But not this time. This time, greater effort only exacerbates the problem.

It's the same with rapport building.

It's a more passive activity than most salespeople are comfortable with or have ever been taught how to do. It's kind of like training a dog to come when it's off leash. If it doesn't come on your call and you run toward it, shouting its name and gesticulating for it to come to you, it runs away. But if instead you turn and walk in the other direction, away from the dog, it will chase you. If you wait for it to get close behind you, you can then turn around and embrace it.

I'm not saying to be coy or run away in the hope the prospective client will chase you and buy, but I am saying that when you run at being accepted too hard, acceptance (rapport) runs the other way.

Going Too Fast

Speed kills! That goes for driving and for rapport building. Let's stay with the driving analogy for a minute.

Let's say you're on a slick, dark, winding, country road in the rain. Is accelerating likely to get you to your destination faster? I'd wager not. In fact I'd wager that accelerating on a dark, undulating, wet roadway is likely to prevent you from getting to your destination at all!

It's that way with rapport. There are no shortcuts. It's about taking the time to take sincere interest in the other person.

Feats

The basis for building rapport is not complex but it takes some practice to do well. And, as noted above, it cannot be achieved in an instant – it takes time. The skill is to ask questions – and not just any questions – and listening to the answers. But the talent is to be sincere – you must be genuine.

Debbie Kosta has honed her skills as a listener so that she can ask the right question at the right time.

EXPERT TAKES

You have to ask difficult questions. I have to build rapport. It's not just talking about the weather. I have to earn the right to probe. I am a risk taker and a little audacious in my questioning. I ask great questions because of the way I ask. Some people want a gentler approach so I have to listen for that. It's a process. I really care about what they're saying, and they feel that.

My *rule* is that I listen to know how to ask and to see if they are ready for a hard question. I have become trained to listen. I respect them, their time, their past and future. I give value before I ask the tough questions. The value may be advice, or it may be a suggestion, but I add value and get an "Oh, wow! She helped me."

I give some of the advice that I learned from Gary Vanyerchuk, Tony Robbins, Jim Rohn, Wayne Dyer etc.

There have been times that I didn't listen right and asked too strong of a question too soon and blew it.

It takes a lot of practice for many, many, years to listen well and earn the right to ask the tough questions.

Asking Questions

I remember when I was a 19-year-old sailor in the United States Navy and my shipmate, Ben, brought me home to visit with his family for the weekend. They were very well off and lived in a beautiful home on a lake. The place was magnificent. The rooms were huge and beautifully appointed. I was a little intimidated having grown up about as far away from wealth and gentility as you can get.

To make matters worse, they sat me next to Ben's dad, the wealthy business guy who had earned all of this opulence. I figured this to be a long night of sitting quietly and staring at my plate until Ben and I could sneak away for some beers. I could not have been more wrong. I ended up in a long conversation with Ben's dad, Mr. Witcher. We spoke for over an hour! When I left his company I was really impressed. I thought Mr. Witcher was easily the nicest, smartest, most sincere guy I'd ever met. I had an awesome time talking with him.

When I reflected on that conversation I realized I knew nothing about the man! Here I was remembering him as the nicest, smartest, most sincere man I'd ever met and the truth was I knew absolutely nothing about him, save that he was Ben's dad. You see, what Mr. Witcher did was to instantly evaluate my discomfort and then proceed to ask me questions about my favorite subject … *me!*

He then *actively* listened to me and continued to prompt me with more questions. He did this so deftly that I never felt interrogated or "on the spot." Instead I felt interesting, understood and well liked. I would imagine this ability to listen well was one of skills that elevated him to become the international president of a major drug company. Having met him for that brief encounter, I can tell you that success was no accident.

Asking questions and listening are the cornerstones of rapport building. Like me at 19, most people are happy to tell you about themselves and having a strategy built around this can really be a blessing in those moments when rapport may seem elusive.

You Can't Fake Sincerity

I remember the conversations I used to have with my wife before we had to attend one of my business functions. Deborah was home raising our girls at the time and always felt a bit out of the loop when it came to business parties. Once or twice a year we would travel on business incentive trips. There was a high degree of togetherness on these trips with many group dinners and tours. My wife would get anxious before we left imagining everyone there would be talking about the business and she would be left out and ignored.

On top of that, I was the VP of sales and the organizer of the trips so, essentially, everyone there reported to me making Deborah "the boss's wife." My position also required me to be on call for people before and during the trip and to take on the MC duties at many of the functions leaving Deborah to fend for herself.

Yet, time after time, I would see her involved in what looked like deep conversations with people. They'd be leaned into one another with earnest expressions, frequent smiles and very open and relaxed body alignment. Invariably, when I went back to the office, I would hear from the folks Deborah had been conversing with. "Oh, my Frank, I had such a good time with your wife." Or "Frank, your wife is awesome. You should bring her around more. We had a great time."

So how did anxious Deborah become the belle of the ball? I was curious as hell about this so I asked. She said she asks questions and listens. "That's it?" I asked.

"Yes," she said. "Mostly about their children. If they don't have kids, I sometimes ask about their relationship – maybe about how they met or something. With some of the younger ones I ask them how they managed to earn the trip."

My wife is a rapport genius!

She asked people about their favorite subjects, themselves or their children, and then let them talk. No wonder they all loved her. The thing was, though, she loved hearing about those things. Deborah could look at pictures of their kids or hear about cute phrases they uttered or what they dressed up as for Halloween all day and be *genuinely* interested in their stories and descriptions. And that was and is an essential key to opening the door to rapport. You've got to be genuine.

> **You've got to be genuine. I remember reading a Kinky Freidman novel many years ago in which he said, "You can't fake sincerity."**

I remember reading a Kinky Freidman novel many years ago in which he said, "You can't fake sincerity." That phrase always stuck with me. I mean Kinky is a world class wise-ass, but think about that a minute. The very definition of sincerity is that it isn't fake. Faking sincerity is a true oxymoron.

Sincerity, genuineness – they both lead to trust. And that, says Peter Chieco, is why people choose to do business with him.

EXPERT TAKES

I have earned their trust. They know I have their best interest in mind and that I am going to work very hard and smart for their benefit. I never really dissected it. I am just the same way all the time to everyone, regardless of account size.

Always be ethical. We don't take short cuts.

We don't work with wholesalers just because they take us to dinner or a ballgame. I always think, what is the benefit for the client? I am looking at the client not focused on my outcome, and that perspective is the key to our success.

So what can we learn from my darling bride? What strategy can we employ in our desire to unleash our sales gene, spike sales, build great relationships and cement long-term loyalty? Well, for starters, *ask questions and listen*. Nobody ever said, "I hate that girl. All she ever does is listen to me!" Let's add to that my wife's sincere interest in other people's kids and their accomplishments. She didn't listen waiting for an opportunity to talk about her own kids. She didn't listen politely, just long enough to excuse herself to move on to another guest. She didn't listen while looking over their shoulder or past them to see what other interesting people might be milling about. And she didn't listen passively. Remember earlier when I said I would see them engaged in deep conversation with their bodies aligned, leaning in toward one another with earnest expressions and frequent smiles? That's called *active listening*.

Active Listening

Debbie Kosta attributes at least part of her success to her ability to listen well and, like my bride, to her genuine interest in people.

EXPERT TAKES

I think that what sets me apart is I respect people and love what I do. Not that they don't; it's just more obvious with me. I come from an honest place. I want to be part of the solution and my sincerity comes through.

I really want to help change the human condition and my business can do that. I am 75-80% referrals. I don't even get leads from the 800 number.

I always ask, "Who do you know who can benefit from this learning the way you did? Who do you know that would, like you, like to add some sunshine into their lives?"

Have you ever accused someone of not listening to you and had them parrot back your last couple of sentences? It's a glib move made to try to prove they were listening but listening and hearing are not the same things.

Active listening is exactly what it says. It requires the listener to be *active*. Active listening employs facial expressions and vocal intonations as well as hand gestures and even light touches to exhibit interest in the speaker. This can mean nodding in acknowledgement. It can mean smiling, or raising your eyebrows in surprise. It can mean a soft touch on the arm or shoulder or actually taking someone's hand. It's grunts, head bobs, appropriate facial expressions, leaning in or out, covering your mouth or slapping a knee. You get what I mean here. Active means action.

Take a moment and picture these anti-listening postures as I name them. You have no doubt experienced most, if not all of them. Remember a time you were speaking to someone and they:

- Looked past you at another person;
- Looked at the TV over the bar;
- Looked at their mobile;
- Looked at their email on the computer screen;
- Looked at their watch;
- Turned slightly away from you;
- Didn't nod or grunt or respond at a point when a nod, grunt or response seemed appropriate;
- Moved their lips while you were speaking as if formulating a response before you completed your sentence (This one infuriates me!);
- Interrupted you; or
- Held a posture that told you, *for sure*, that they were just waiting for you to take a breath so they could speak.

Really bring up one of these images. Sit in it for a moment. Make it as real as you can. See what you saw, feel what you felt, hear what you heard. Put down the book or the tablet for a minute; close your eyes and really relive it. How did you feel? Disrespected? Disliked? Marginalized? Beside the point? This is what I want you to remember; that feeling.

Depending on the listener and their model of the world, you can lose rapport in a split second by executing one of these, seemingly, benign moves and often you won't even know you dropped a notch on the esteem scale of the person you're speaking with.

ACTIVE LISTENING

- Good eye contact.
- Eye movement. Squinting and wide-eyed, as appropriate.
- Facial expressions that convey understanding.
- Nodding.
- Eyebrow flashes.
- "Ahh"s and "um hmm"s; grunting where a grunt conveys understanding.
- Leaning in.
- Light touches on the forearm, hand or shoulder.

We've discussed briefly the science behind better communication and we have some guidelines on approaches to avoid and styles to develop in order to communicate better, to build rapport and solidify relationships. But are there some tried and true tips and strategies to connect and bond? Of course there are.

As Julie Andrews so beautifully sang in *The Sound of Music*, "Let's start at the very beginning, a very good place to start."

CHAPTER 7

Rapport in the Beginning

How do you meet someone? I don't mean find out who the head of Goldman Sachs is and get a meeting, I mean the physical meeting of someone new.

Most of us pay little attention to this. After all, we've met hundreds of people; done this our entire lives. Joe introduces us to Jennifer and we give a quick shake and mutter something like "Hello" or "It's nice to meet you." Then, eight out of ten times we forget her name and, if questioned, could not recount the color or her eyes, if Jennifer had a necklace on or even whether or not she wore glasses.

We take meeting folks for granted – *and that's a mistake*. This is where rapport begins and it is your first opportunity to be well thought of.

The Conscious Greeting

Surely you've heard the expression that you only get one chance to make a first impression? So why don't we pay closer attention to this critical moment? Beginning now, you will because I am going to give you a very simple system to be sure you make a great first impression every time.

Have you ever met someone you had a bad feeling about from the start? Why do you think that is? Let me tell you. You calibrated a bunch of infinitesimal facial and body cues and drew a subconscious conclusion in under 2 seconds. You likely could not identify all of the subtle cues that led you to that quick judgment but I can tell you it was some combination of body alignment, eye contact, touch, micro-expressions and sound.

This is how you *consciously* meet someone. Let me break it down.

Be Wide Open

At the very moment of introduction, face the person, heart to heart. You need to be wide open. That means your arms are relaxed and either alongside or outside of your frame. Hands in front of you, before leading to a handshake, is a closed posture and inhibits rapport.

Remember, just above, when I talked about meeting someone and calibrating various cues to come to a quick "I don't like/trust this person" judgment? One of the things that could have been wrong was body alignment. Maybe they came in with their side leading. Maybe they looked away. Perhaps they had their hands in front, like a shield, just before reaching in for a handshake. All of these postures are instantly calculated and subconsciously judged.

Think about it. We are descended from cave dwellers. When a caveman approached any other living creature, he had to first decide if this being was a danger to him. How do you think he did that? He read the body language. We still do this.

We do it consciously and overtly, like changing sides of the street when a drug-addled, homeless person is ranting their way up the sidewalk toward us. We see possible danger and move. We also do this unconsciously and less obviously, like meeting someone who violates one of the steps I am giving you now.

The next step for our prehistoric ancestor was to evaluate whether the being in front of him was a foe, a friend or a possible mate and that instant judgment came from calibrating the posture of the being before him. Beyond those three categories he had little interest. It has been about two hundred thousand years since then, but hit the bar scene in any metropolis and you'll notice that things have not evolved all that much, have they?

Soft Eye Contact

So getting back to our meeting criteria, once we present ourselves physically wide open, aiming our heart at their heart, the very next thing to do is make soft eye contact. Soften your eyes by focusing on how really nice it is to meet this person; be totally present. Make eye contact for a moment – not ten moments locked in like you're trying to read her inner most thoughts. We have a word in modern society for people who hold eye contact too long. Creepster!

Making soft eye contact incorporates a three-part move. As you make eye contact, smile and add a quick eyebrow flash, accompanied by a brief greeting.

1. Smile
2. Eyebrow Flash
3. Greeting

The smile says, "Welcome. I am really happy to meet you. I have time for this meeting and am where I am right now." A smile also helps to soften the eyes. The eyebrow flash is a brief lifting of the brows as you smile. It instantly tells the subconscious, "This person is friendly." Then, say "hello" or "nice to meet you" or whatever greeting you're comfortable with as you reach to shake hands.

While all aspects of the greeting are critical, I want to emphasize soft eye contact. At the various seminars and keynote talks I give, I get to meet a lot of people. There is a bit of celebrity involved in that I am the advertised and featured speaker and people want to see me up close and personal either before or after I present. Because of that slight bit of celebrity, I give extra focus to this part of the greeting. I do this because people are often unsure of themselves when they approach. They wonder if they are welcome or if they are interrupting. A lack of focus on my part, during this critical moment of our greeting, would marginalize them. It would make them feel as though I don't really have time for them or that I'm too full of myself to give them my attention.

You see, they're coming to the encounter with a preconceived notion that I am up on stage and they are down below in the audience and that means there is a separation between us. The slightest miscue by me – not making eye contact well or seeming preoccupied or rushed – will fulfill the preconceived notion of "I guess he's just too wrapped up in himself to meet me." I mention this because folks come to you with prejudicial views as well. Sometimes they've had a few minutes to observe you before the introduction and they've formed an opinion as to who and what you are. They come to the meeting with a predetermined opinion in the front of their minds just waiting for you to fulfill it.

Perhaps you're in a position of authority and someone comes to the greeting slightly intimidated. It could even be that you've encountered someone while you're dressed and ready for the day, but they're in sweats, with bed hair, heading to the gym. This moment of soft eye contact and the sincere conveyance of how pleased you are to meet them is critical and can overcome any mistaken notions or discomfort with the moment they may have.

The Handshake

First, let me do a brief commercial on the handshake.

You don't need to show me how hard you're hitting the gym by trying to break the 28 bones in my hand. Nor do I want a limp, dishrag shake. Like *Goldilocks and the Three Bears*, your handshake should be not too hard, not too soft, just right.

One other warning to the men out there. When you shake a woman's hand, shake it as you would a man's, albeit a bit gentler. I see guys grabbing the tips of a woman's fingers like a knight returning a handkerchief to a fair maiden. The woman you're being introduced to is a business associate or social acquaintance of some kind, not foreign royalty! Shake her hand! It's at the least insulting but assuredly borderline misogynistic to shake her hand like she's less than you.

It's at the least insulting but assuredly borderline misogynistic to shake a woman's hand like she's less than you. Shake her hand!

The last thing on the handshake is this. Do overs, like we had in the schoolyard as kids, are totally fair. If you go to shake a hand and physically miss connecting, don't sit in that awkward moment knowing you both feel a little weird. Own it! Put on a big smile and say, "Hey, I think we missed that one. Let's try again and have a proper handshake." You will feel better, they will be relieved and you will have gotten off on the right foot with an extra bit of rapport built in.

Finally, there are a couple of points in making a proper handshake. Lean in just a tad. Don't go so far as to invade their space, but leaning in a bit conveys warmth and intimacy. Once the introductory handshake is over, stay squared up and open, heart to heart, and repeat the person's name back to them and then a to yourself. Anchoring the name consciously at the moment of introduction will keep it from sliding out of your head 5 seconds after you hear it.

These small, seemingly unnoticeable body moves make a huge difference. Twenty-first century humans still have a lot of ancestral DNA that comes, subconsciously, to bear and you don't want to be ill thought of right out of the blocks because your attention was diverted and you offered a half-turned body, with a half-hearted greeting at the first meeting.

HOW TO IMPLANT A NAME

When I meet someone and they tell me their name, I immediately repeat it back. "Tiffany? It's so nice to meet you Tiffany."

Then I look at her, making eye contact, smiling and in a nano-second, while I focus on that face, I say to myself "Tiffany, Tiffany, She's Tiffany" anchoring the name to the face. Sometimes I make an association like if she has big earrings or a pronounced necklace I will sing to myself "with a little box from Tiffany" from the Christmas song "Santa Baby."

Or maybe I meet Rich and I say to myself "Richie Rich" while evoking an image of him at the head of an impossibly long table like a scene from that movie.

One last example is the Rhyme. I met Cassie in the gym and when I looked at her I said "Sassy Cassie" to myself a few times. When I see her Sassy Cassie jumps in to my head far faster than just plain Cassie would have.

So in the end, you are following seven simple steps when you consciously meet someone.

1. Be open; heart to heart.
2. Make soft eye contact with a quick flash of the eyebrows.
3. Smile.
4. Offer a greeting.
5. Reach for a proper handshake.
6. Lean in a bit.
7. Say their name back to them and again to yourself.

Assuming you have done the meeting part well, you are now on the way to gaining rapport. As we discussed at the beginning of this Part (see Chapters 5 and 6), going further and building a relation-ship involves having a conversation, a real conversation. So let's go further, let's talk about some other methods you can employ as you make a deeper connection.

CHAPTER 8

Watch Those Feet!

I took an audio training class in body language some years back. The instructor was an FBI agent named Joe Navarro. Joe told us that the feet are an often overlooked, but excellent, source of feedback. The quote I remember is "The feet never lie."

Lessons from an FBI Agent

Joe gave a few examples of feet as a harbinger and one I remember well is that the feet lead the way. If you see someone *in* a conversation but their feet are pointing *out* of the conversation, you can bet that conversation won't be long lived. In other words, when you're speaking to someone who is ready to end the chat, often that person's foot will turn away from you before the person does.

Another foot lesson I learned from Joe is that in an uncertain situation we humans keep both feet firmly planted on the ground at about shoulder width, so that we are centered. This is a ready position to fend off an attack and is hard wired into our lizard brain from Neanderthal times. Of course, we have evolved a lot and are not likely to get shoved in a business or social encounter but, still, our bodies remember this programming and use it all the time.

> **The feet lead the way. Someone truly engaged *in* a conversation will have their feet pointing toward their discussion partner, but if their feet are pointing *out* of the conversation, they are ready to end the chat.**

The next time you are in an elevator notice that people who do not have their back to a wall are unlikely to have crossed feet. Crossed feet is the opposite of squared up; it's a vulnerable position and one we only take when we are comfortable with the people we are in close proximity with or speaking to. Picture it. If you were shoved or attacked in any way, crossed feet would make you fall over, whereas firmly planted, squared-up feet are more likely to allow you to keep your balance.

I remember when I first learned this concept. Like any new learning, I was fascinated with finding examples and paid attention as I went through my days. Of course, the power of selective attention[3] was now in play and I was as fixated on shoes like I was Imelda Marcos.

The Foot Experiment

One night, as I attended a business mixer, I ran into an associate from my industry. Barbara was a 40-something professional who was enjoying a very successful, 20-year career in equipment sales. She and I had known one another for a few years and had gotten along famously from the start since we were both career salespeople with very similar levels of experience.

As Barbara and I stood facing each other and chatting, I noticed that she crossed her feet in a very relaxed position, ankle over ankle. Remembering my instructor's words about the feet I knew this meant she was very comfortable with me. So, I set out to ruin that.

Embarking on my own little experiment, I pointed my foot away from Barbara as though I was readying myself to leave. In a beat, she uncrossed her feet. I squared up, smiled and once again pointed both of my feet in her direction. She smiled back and crossed her feet again. We spoke for a few minutes and I did it again, pointed my foot away. Guess what? She instantly uncrossed her feet!

This amazed me! I mean I knew Joe was an FBI expert but to see it in action and so obvious was mind blowing! I am sorry to say that to this day, I have no idea what Barbara and I spoke about. Being the body language novice that I was, I was unable to take in the feet peripherally while giving my focused attention to Barbara. But the lesson of that day stands out in my mind and I use this example in my seminars – the feet never lie.

CHAPTER 9

Conversational Tools

Two great tools for building rapport are *backtracking* and *mirroring*. Both are conversational tools that should be used sparingly. And like many of the methods we've discussed, these techniques take time and practice to develop.

It's like learning to ride a bike. Once you have it, you become unconsciously competent; you don't have to think about it, you just ride. But on the way to riding mastery there will be few skinned knees, bruised elbows and scratched bike frames. These particular tactics can definitely cause bruising.

Both backtracking and mirroring must become as natural as riding a bike, just be careful not to bruise a friend, family member or business associate as you learn.

Backtracking

Sometimes people are reticent to share what's really going on. The conversation never gets past surface skimming. Conversations like that don't build trust or rapport. Backtracking is a technique to help to get someone to open up a bit.

Backtracking is a wonderful tool to elicit more information. Sometimes people you encounter have a difficult time offering you a complete story or sometimes the story is actually buried under the surface of what they're saying.

Backtracking is a great way to help them get unstuck. It is simply repeating the last few words someone says back to them with a bit of a question tone at the end. Here is a mock conversation to serve as an example.

Backtracking in Action

Todd and Tracy are dating. They meet for a drink and Todd notices that Tracy looks a bit out of sorts. Nothing too overt, just off a bit. Todd knows Tracy isn't one to easily share her feelings so he employs backtracking.

TODD: Tracy, are you okay?

TRACY: Fine.

TODD: What did you do today?

TRACY: I went to the park.

TODD: Went to the park?

TRACY: Yeah, I wanted some quiet time.

TODD: Quiet time?

TRACY: Yeah, I had a fight with my mom and she really hurt my feelings.

TODD: Wow, it sucks that she *hurt your feelings*.

TRACY: Yeah. She said I don't pay her enough attention but I'm the only one who goes there to help her. Why does she always favor my sister? Sue never does anything! She's been the golden child my whole life!

Let's look at how this conversation could have gone had Todd's first response to the park been, "That's nice; did you enjoy the park?"

TODD: Tracy, are you okay?

TRACY: Fine.

TODD: What did you do today?

TRACY: I went to the park.

TODD: That's nice. Did you enjoy the park?

TRACY: It was Okay.

TODD: I took my dog there last week. He loved it

TRACY: That's cool.

TODD: I'm glad they provide those bags to pick up after your dog; that's convenient

TRACY: Yup, sure is.

He wouldn't have found out about the fight with Tracy's mom nor would he have learned about Tracy's view that her sister was always favored. Isn't this a pretty important part of Tracy's life story?

So what's the point? Couldn't Todd have asked how Tracy is and couldn't Tracy have said "Fine," like millions of others say millions of times a day? Couldn't the conversation have gone the way of our second example very easily? And while that may be fine some of the time, after this bit of sharing how do you think Tracy feels about Todd?

This is the goal in a sales relationship, or for that matter any relationship, isn't it? Don't you want to be liked and trusted? Backtracking is just one of the tools you can bring to bear to help you to gain rapport.

Cautionary Tale

I would like to offer a caution here since this just happened to me at a recent seminar. These are *tools*. They need to be used in the right *situation* and in the right *proportion*. I have over tightened many a screw in my day and the result was a broken screw head and lots of additional time to reverse the damage and begin again. It's like that with backtracking.

A woman at a seminar I recently led told me that she tried backtracking and it backfired! Upon further examination, I learned that she jumped into it (I was really proud of her for trying) with her husband. She backtracked him for three or four sentences in a row. He looked at her and said, "What the hell are you doing repeating everything I say?" She over tightened the screw until it broke.

Go back to the conversation above and see how gently Todd employed the technique. Also realize this isn't someone he knows intimately; it's someone he *wants* to know intimately. Trying to backtrack your spouse, especially for so many sentences in a row, is a huge pattern interruption and likely to feel wrong, like it did to the seminar woman's husband.

Being married, their conversations were comfortable and followed their peculiar pattern of language. Backtracking him so aggressively was akin to her dyeing her hair green and sitting down to dinner in a bikini. Definitely out of the norm and very noticeable.

The communication tools I'm offering are meant to be subtle and seamless, like highlights in your hair or a new blouse; an enhancement that will bring greater attention and appeal but not likely to stick out like green hair and a bikini.

SOME RULES FOR BACKTRACKING

- Use to help someone get unstuck.
- Use to help someone go a bit deeper.
- Use sparingly in a conversation.
- Don't mimic.
- Repeat the last couple of words and, sometimes, add a word or two.
- Repeat those last couple of words with a questioning inflection or one of astonishment.

Mirroring

Another communication tool for building rapport is mirroring. Mirroring is exactly what it sounds like: subtly imitating the physical posture and movements of the person you're speaking with.

This is not monkey see monkey do. You don't want to overtly imitate every move your partner makes. Instead, notice their body posture first. Are they sitting with their feet flat on the floor or cross legged? Are they leaning on the arm of the chair or sitting back? Sit the way they're sitting. Perhaps they shift some and lean forward. Wait a bit and lean in yourself. If you see them moving a hand to their face, leaning their chin on their fist, wait a bit and make a similar move.

Again, the same warning as above. This isn't mimicry; it is subtle, similar body matching. What you're doing is front-ending rapport. When people are in deep rapport, they often move and position their bodies in similar ways. In fact, I have heard that some long-term couples in deep rapport even breathe at the same rate while sleeping! By doing this upfront, you are telling your partner's subconscious that you are already in rapport, that you are likeable and trustworthy because you are in the posture that a longtime friend might take with him/her.

> **Warning: This isn't mimicry; it is subtle, similar body matching.**

Understand what's going on with people who are in rapport. Their subconscious is constantly seeking similarities between them. It is continually looking for ways to make them more alike. Each subconscious seeks to refashion the vocal, physical and emotional patterns to be more like the one they are amorous of. Having this awareness allows you to fast-track rapport and get yourself in a position to help (sell).

Mirroring in Action

You have likely seen this more obviously with kids because they aren't coy or self-conscious about it.

I remember when I was 11 years of age. I had been raised in New York City my entire life and had the commensurate NY city accent. My dad's best friend, known to my siblings and me as Uncle Conrad, moved his family to Los Angeles and we drove out there to visit. We spent 3 weeks at their house. Uncle Conrad had four kids of similar ages to my brother, sister and me and we spent 24/7 with our "cousins" for those 3 weeks.

This was 1969. Johnny Cash was all over the radio with "A Boy Named Sue," Taco Bell was the fast-growing, west-coast answer to McDonalds and the cool expression of the day was "That's Boss!" As New Yorkers we pronounced it "Baws," the "o" sound as used in "ought." The California kids said, "Bas," using the "a" sound as it's used in "pasta."

One day, at the beach, my dad overheard me say, "That's Bas," just the way they did. He looked at me quizzically and said, "Why you talking like them? You ain't from here."

What happened, dear father, was rapport. I couldn't explain it then, but this was my little subconscious trying to make me similar to the people I liked. My brother, sister and I had taken on the speech, and probably the behavioral patterns, of our Beach Boy loving cousins. Our subconscious was working overtime teaching us how to be more like the people we liked and whom we wanted to like us.

This kind of mimicry is the natural result of good rapport you see in best friends and longtime couples – even sometimes with people and their dogs!

Assuming Rapport

What I am suggesting with mirroring and backtracking is to *assume rapport*; acting the way one would act if they were already in a good, trusted position with the person they are interacting.

As a salesperson, fundraiser, boss or convincer of any kind, it is incumbent upon you to create rapport. You have been in good rapport many times before. You have no doubt "clicked" with certain people throughout your life and have found yourself in great rapport with others after some time. But you likely don't know how it happened, what the mechanics of it were.

What you're learning here is how to reverse engineer those relationships and those moments so that you can reconstruct them, at will, to gain rapport quickly and intentionally rather than haphazardly over time.

This is very powerful juju but, again, don't move too quickly and don't try it with green hair and a bikini at dinner.

CHAPTER 10

Behavioral Tools

While communication skills will bring you a long way in building rapport, they alone are not enough. It is just as important to develop strong behavioral awareness and techniques.

Pacing and Leading

I remember well the day I took my 16-year-old daughter to visit a talent agent. Alicia aspired, at that time, to be an actress. She has a natural ability to get up on stage and command the attention of any room. She can sing and dance and, Daddy bias aside, she is gorgeous. We were fortunate to have become friendly with the great actor, Tony Lo Bianco, who subsequently recommended this particular agent and set up the meeting.

Let me set the scene. We enter an apartment/office that is a little dark and subdued. The colors are all rather muted, and adding to the meditative atmosphere are dark and heavy draperies on the windows. There is a couch in front of us covered with large pillows and throw blankets. The woman who greets us is dressed very much like the decor in the room – soft, quiet and comfortable. She moves slowly as she guides us to the couch. There is a coffee table loaded with books and papers and an armchair to our left that looks like a shortened version of the couch. She takes the chair, we take the couch with Alicia closest to her.

The conditions I just described tell me that this woman is, what we refer to in neuro-linguistic programming (NLP), a kinesthetic or a feelings-based communicator.[4] When you think of a kinesthetic, think of comfortable and leisurely in terms of their approach and pace to life.

Now juxtapose this with my daughter. She is very athletic, brightly clad and highly verbal. To borrow a line from the great Zig Ziglar, Alicia has been known to speak at about 200 words per minute with gusts of up to 500. She is definitely a visual communicator.

The kinesthetic woman, sitting back in her chair, began to speak about the travails of pursuing life on the stage. To show that she totally understood, Alicia leaned forward and, beaming, related at a rapid pace to what the agent was saying a nano-second after the woman had said it.

The metaphoric crash was devastating with throw pillows, comforters and brightly colored Barbie clothes strewn about the accident scene — at least that's what I saw in my mind.

What actually happened was the agent sat back further, practically disappearing into her chair as she spoke softly in slow, emphatic, measured sentences in an attempt to be understood. Alicia continued to lean forward, smile and jump on the end of every sentence, rapidly trying to convey that she understood completely and could connect with what the woman was saying.

I think you get the picture here. Alicia sensed she was not in rapport which caused her to try harder. Trying harder for Alicia meant leaning further in, animating herself more and speaking faster and louder in an effort to penetrate the wall she was sensing she had to break through. I wish I could say I jumped in and saved the day but I didn't. The meeting ended and we left knowing we would never hear from the agent but Alicia went on to a wonderful career as a yoga instructor and health coach. What can I say, who knows what they really want to do at 16?

Reading the Situation

Getting back to our point, though, pacing and leading are a huge part of gaining rapport. If Alicia had known this she would have sat back and listened, pausing for a beat or two before she replied to anything. Further, she would have slowed her own speech pattern down a bit to match the pattern of the agent, thus, making her feel more comfortable.

In this situation Alicia is the salesperson. She is seeking something from the agent. It is incumbent upon Alicia to facilitate the communication. Remember, *you are responsible for the results of your encounters?* In this instance, Alicia walked away without getting what she'd come for. She could talk about the woman being weird or off-putting or less than friendly and, so what? She left without getting what she came for; she didn't make the sale.

Meeting someone where they are and noticing their pace and tone are essential to gaining rapport and having meaningful communication.

Meeting someone where they are and noticing their pace and tone are essential to gaining rapport and having meaningful communication. I remember a scene in *Natural Born Killers* when Juliette Lewis goes into a car repair garage and hits on the mechanic. She sidles up next to him and begins to kiss and touch him. He immediately "jumps her bones" and exuberantly starts tearing off his clothes and hers in an effort to get to the sex as quickly as he can. She pushes him away and shoots him dead. Then she looks down at him and says, "Next time don't be so effing eager." Being too effing eager, as I said, is a killer.

Paying attention to and matching pace and tone are a great start on the road to rapport. Once you're in sync, you can actually lead someone to a more comfortable pace for you – but getting in sync is essential.

Besides reflective, visual, auditory and kinesthetic, there are other components to personality style that need to be considered. To varying degrees, people are either matchers or mismatchers. That is, they lean toward finding similarities or finding differences with the world around them. While matchers may seem easier to build rapport and gain agreement with both styles need to be recognized and given attention.

Matchers and Mismatchers

My former boss, Joe Weiss, is the guy who introduced me to NLP. Joe had a watershed moment of his own that caused him to seek out a better understanding of human communication.

He'd been blindsided by the abrupt end of a long relationship. Joe was a successful entrepreneur. His company was growing and his employees seemed very invested. Joe wasn't an "ivory tower" type of boss. He was always out among the employees listening to issues and offering help. It was the same in his life outside of work. Joe was generous with his time and was sought out by his friends for his soft ear and sound advice. He was everyone's "Dutch uncle," helping friends to examine situations and offering his wisdom and experience freely. As a result, Joe was especially hard on himself for not having been more aware of the depth of trouble in his own romantic relationship.

Joe was a lifelong learner and a big believer in personal responsibility. He looked back at his relationship and, although in hindsight he was able to see some cues he might have picked up sooner, he felt as though he had missed too many signs. Joe wanted to improve upon his ability to listen well and understand, to see beyond what was obvious in any communication. So, he enrolled in the New York NLP Institute.

He took to NLP like a fish takes to water; he loved it. In fact Joe not only became a master practitioner of NLP, he was so good at it that he was invited to train instructors so that they could become certified to teach this great communications science. It was Joe who taught me this amazing concept of matchers and mismatchers.

The Matchers

Whenever I give a talk and even in casual conversation, I immediately recognize the matchers. As I speak they occasionally nod their heads up and down in a "yes" motion, signaling that they understand what I am saying and they identify similarities in their stored experiences with what I am saying. Matchers are people who look for sameness. They're relaters. When you tell a matcher something that happened to you, they think of something similar that happened to them and relate it back to you. Matchers match.

This does not mean that they always agree with you, but they look to find similarities in your experience and theirs to help them to make sense of whatever you are relating to them. Matchers, at their extreme end, can frustrate you. Sometimes the need to relate and find sameness is too strong and they don't offer real opinions, just agreement.

The Mismatchers

Mismatchers, on the other hand, look to change what they see and hear. They look to put their own touch on it rather than relate sameness. Mismatchers are often looked at as negative people because of this need to find and display difference, but they are mostly creative people looking to make improvements to whatever they see and hear. When they listen to ideas or look at projects their brains are processing it all through their own particular lens. They're thinking about how to adjust things more to their way. Sometimes it is creative. Sometimes it is just change for the sake of change – to make it their own. It depends on the level of social development here. There is a fine line between creative license and insult.

If I drive into a parking lot with a mismatcher and go to pull into a space on the left, the mismatcher says, "Why don't you park here, on the right?" In these moments I wish I had a big God clock so that I could stop the action and turn it back 3 seconds to begin to turn my wheel to park on right just so I could hear them say, "No, why don't you park on the left?"

Again, God's cruel joke is at play here. If you are in a committed relationship it is highly likely that you are one of these and your significant other is, well, the other.

> **God's cruel joke is at play here. If you are in a committed relationship it is highly likely that you are one of these — a matcher or a mismatcher — and your significant other is, well, the other.**

Another Difference

Another way to recognize matchers and mismatchers is by a simple yes or no test.

As a matcher myself I have had to train myself to say no. People ask me for something and my immediate response is "Yes, I can do that." Matchers, in an effort to match, agree too quickly and then have regret later as they find themselves over committed or committed to a task or event they would really rather not do. I teach matchers to pause at the moment of the ask and literally ask themselves, "Why shouldn't I agree to do this?" before they agree to anything.

This really bears fruit for a matcher in a sales situation or negotiation. The tendency to agree too readily can hurt you in a few ways. One is obviously that you can lose precious ground in a negotiation by agreeing too quickly. Another is that in a sales situation saying yes too quickly can get you into "over promise and under deliver" territory when what you want is the exact opposite of that. You always want to deliver beyond the expectations of your client.

Another downside to matching too quickly with a client is that sometimes you agree to something that is likely but not definite, like a color choice, delivery date or an exception from management. If these things do not happen, the client is disappointed and that situation could have been avoided with a simple "I may be able to get that done for you but I have to make a call to be certain. May I get back to you on that?"

Mismatchers have a tendency to say no out of hand. But the no isn't always a no. Mismatchers need more time to process, to turn the ask into something they have a thumbprint on, something that will work for them. A flat out yes is scary for a mismatcher. They didn't get a chance to go in and monkey around with your request. One of the worst things you can do with a mismatcher is to challenge that out-of-hand no. It's better to let it steep, understanding that the no is often just buying time to think. If you challenge the no right away, the mismatcher will probably dig their heels in and solidify that no right then and there.

Remember that few people are extremely one side or the other. Most folks have some balance, but keep your eyes out for those who lean heavily one way or the other.

Managing Each Style

Matchers don't require any special handling. Just don't think you're going to get real feedback without specifically asking. Show a matcher your new haircut and she will say, "I like it. It looks kind of like Jennifer Lawrence in *The Hunger Games*." Ask a mismatcher and you'll either get, "It's nice but I liked it better longer" or "I wouldn't have cut it so short." So what does that mean to us day to day?

If you're working on a project and look at your progress with either of these two personalities, you need to manage the outcome you want. With matchers you need to use positive language to invite them to offer suggestions. With a matcher, for example, you might ask, "Tell me what you would like to see changed here?" Or ask specific questions like, "What color schemes would work for better you?" Remember a matcher seeks sameness and wants to agree. If you say, "Do you like the color scheme?" The answer will likely be yes. If you ask what color scheme will work better for you? You will get them thinking beyond yes.

> **With matchers you need to use positive language to invite them to offer suggestions. With mismatchers, you've got to use a lot of negative language to get a positive outcome.**

With mismatchers, you've got to use a lot of negative language to get a positive outcome. They speak in "no"s, "not"s, "can't"s, "won't"s and "don't"s. Mismatchers come in various degrees of severity. I used to manage a team with a guy who is what I refer to as a "knee-jerk mismatcher." He literally begins sentences with the word "no." A conversation with him about an employee might go like this.

HIM: I don't think Phil is going to work out here. He doesn't have a sense of urgency.

ME: I know what you mean. I had to remind him a few times about a 911 on one of my biggest accounts to get him to respond.

HIM: No, I mean, he just doesn't get it. He can't even reply to an important email.

ME: I agree. He is definitely slow on the uptake.

HIM: No, it's really bad. I called him this morning and it's already noon, and he still hasn't gotten back to me.

Do you see the futility of me trying to match a mismatcher? He literally will not allow me to agree with him. He says Phil is slow, I agree and I add an example of my own about Phil's slowness, and his next sentence begins with "No," implying that I am not on the same page. He does this because as an *extreme* mismatcher, he needs to constantly reject any statement but his. He wants to retool *my* words to better convey *his* understanding of the situation. In this case it is only my frustration that is at stake. We both agree Phil is not a fit for us so the fact that he cannot let me agree bothers me only in my recognition of the broken communication.

But what if I didn't agree? What if I think Phil is capable of improvement and just needs to be coached some. Since he is a knee-jerk mismatcher, I cannot come to Phil's defense without burying Phil even deeper because, as I try to state anything good about Phil, he has to say the opposite. If I did try this with no knowledge of how to manage a conversation with a mismatcher, it would look like this.

HIM: I don't think Phil is going to work out here. He doesn't have a sense of urgency.

ME: I don't know, I have had some good results with him. I think he's coachable.

HIM: No way, he is not. I tried to coach him. I called him out on this a few times. Even Michelle and Sandy said he doesn't respond to emails.

ME: I'm not really having that same experience with Phil. I will meet with him.

HIM: No, it's really bad. I called him this morning and it's already noon, and he still hasn't gotten back to me. We have to let him go today.

Instead, if I want to take a shot at saving Phil, I would have to handle the conversation like this.

HIM: I don't think Phil is going to work out here. He doesn't have a sense of urgency.

ME: Right, should I bring him in now and fire him?

HIM: No. I mean, he needs to respond more quickly.

ME: Won't happen. He has not been responsive to anyone.

HIM: No, it's not that the department won't run. I just need him to liven up and be quicker.

ME: You don't want me to write him up do you?

HIM: Yes, give him a written warning.

ME: Okay, I will meet with him.

Behavioral tools require observation first – observing the environment, looking for clues in the dress and general manner of the other person, scrutinizing the other person's behavior. Next is your response to these cues. How do you build rapport and create a deeper connection?

CHAPTER 11

Calibration

In my seminars I often grab a volunteer and put them in the front of the room as my model. I ask them to think of two people. One that they love with all of their heart and one that they loathe.

Then, while they face the group, I say, "Of the two people you have in your mind, which one is taller?" The audience and I wait a beat and watch the volunteer.

"Which one lives closer to you?" Again, we wait a few seconds as we watch the volunteer.

"Which one is older?" and so on.

They speak no words, they just think of the one who is taller, lives closer, etc. The group, almost 100% of the time, knows whether the love or loathe relationship is taller, lives closer, etc. That is calibration.

Calibration is the process of finding a relationship between quantities that are unknown. For our purposes that means micro-expressions. It means that after a good bit of observation we assign quantities to some of the physical signs we detect during a conversation.

For example, if I am speaking to a very fair-skinned person who shows a color flush at the slightest sign of discomfort, I would not assign the same value to a flush I see on someone with a darker complexion who has to feel very strong emotion in order for color to show in his neck or cheeks. Calibrating physical cues in a person is about seeing the cue – a color flush – in relation to the emotion expressed or the situation described to understand the relationship that particular cue has to the depth of emotion the individual is reacting to.

This information, as you go forward, can help you to gain rapport when, for example, someone exhibits the physical cue without speaking. Great poker players do something similar to this called looking for "tells," which are physical ticks that reveal a particular feeling in an opponent. It is reading nuances in the color, breathing, body posture and facial expressions of the person you are communicating with.

Achieving Unconscious Competence

The thing with calibration is this. You need to get to the level of unconscious competence to use this well. Learning takes place in four steps.[5]

1. Unconscious incompetence: You don't know that you don't know.
2. Conscious incompetence: You know that you don't know. You become aware of something you want to learn.
3. Conscious competence: You know that you know. You've learned something and are doing it.
4. Unconscious competence: This is mastery. You do it without thinking. Like moving your foot from the gas to the brake pedal to slow down.

Remember my story about Barbara in Chapter 9? Remember how I was so intrigued with the foot movement? I was consciously competent. I knew what the feet could tell me but I was so focused on this new bit of learning that I lost the conversation. Unconscious competence with Barbara would have meant I took the foot movement in peripherally without losing focus on the conversation.

Again, like driving a car, I am focused on the road but move from the gas to the brake seamlessly as part of the overall picture in response to what I take in from all around me. I don't think, "There is an animal in the street. Let me lift my foot from the gas pedal and move it over to the brake." I just do it.

In terms of calibration, matching, mirroring, foot movement, language preferences, etc., all of this needs to get to the mastery level to be really useful.

Mastering Calibration

CALIBRATION

Calibration is the overall assessment of all of these cues and more. Don't be daunted by the idea of trying to see so many things while you are focusing on the conversation. With practice you will learn to take them all in unconsciously, and gut-assess what they mean all together.

This is what it is like with calibration. Remember back in Chapter 5, when I told you the story of Jimmy and me walking into the office and greeting Michelle? Jimmy picked up on the fact that Michelle was distressed while I said hello and she said hello back and I saw nothing wrong.

Jimmy *calibrated masterfully* in that moment. He said hello and as he looked at her he unconsciously, and very competently, quantified a variety of little cues to come to the conclusion that Michelle was in distress.

It could have been that she looked away too quickly or there was a flush of color in her cheeks. It may have been that her breathing looked high and shallow or that she held a hand at her throat. Maybe the lines next to her eyes or mouth were slightly more pronounced or her shoulders drooped. I don't know, but I do know that some combination of those cues or others were instantly, unconsciously and competently calibrated by Jimmy to trigger something in his brain that said, "Michelle needs help."

Caveat to Note

One more warning on using these techniques. Alfred Korzybski said, "The map is not the territory."[6] He meant that there is a difference between belief and reality. The way this pertains to us is to be mindful that not everything we see means what we may think it means. No, I did not just throw the baby out with the bathwater. The science behind what we are studying here in body language and calibration is certainly valid. My caution with Mr. Korzybski's quote is that not every display of crossed arms means disinterest.

In other words, calibration is a process of estimating and building. Slightly slumped shoulders don't always mean depression. I would have to assess more of the body posture, the eye movements, the vocal tone and pace and the rate of breathing before I concluded that depression might be a factor.

When we calibrate we are not making snap judgments. We are taking in more than the obvious indicators (words) to help us to gain a fuller understanding of where the other person is emotionally, and then using that information to help us to meet them there and gain rapport.

I cannot state the central idea of all of this enough. In order to succeed at anything in life you will need to work with other people. Unless you can communicate your message clearly, understand and be understood, those other people may hinder rather than help you. Easing into rapport intentionally, with the skills I'm showing you here, will help you to achieve the things you set out to achieve and will help to ensure that the people you encounter along the way will open doors for you.

**Easing into rapport intentionally,
with the skills I'm showing you here,
will help you to achieve the things you
set out to achieve and will help to ensure
that the people you encounter along
the way will open doors for you.**

Way back in the early 90s when my interest in NLP was just beginning to bud, I had a conversation with a Master Practitioner of NLP. He was an instructor at the NLP Center of New York and the person who was responsible for introducing me to this great, life-changing science to begin with.

I had been struggling a bit with my eldest daughter Christine. Let me explain. We joke about Christine, calling her Mary Poppins, "Practically perfect in every way." Christine was a model child. She took care of her little sister, was very respectful, got good grades in school, cleaned her room, helped her mom and me and did it all happily. So what problem could I have been having? I couldn't make her cry. Let me explain.

I'm a big loud NY Italian, not very different in voice and mannerisms than the guys you saw in *GoodFellas* or on *The Sopranos*. When I verbally disciplined my 8-year-old daughter, I expected to see contrition in the way little girls usually exhibit contrition, a flood of tears followed by "I'm sorry Daddy." Then we hug, I forgive her and all is good. What I got instead was a stoic face, maybe downcast eyes and silence.

This problem came up one day while I was speaking with Joe, the master practitioner I mentioned. I told him that Christine had forgotten to do a homework assignment and received a zero for it. When I learned that she'd been in her room listening to music the night before, rather than doing the assignment, I dressed her down but, as I said, saw no remorse. Not seeing the reaction I wanted and expected I became more demonstrative and my voice got louder. But I only got the downcast look. Frustrated, I doled out some lame punishment, like no TV for a few days or something, and stormed off.

Joe asked me about Christine's personality and specifically about Christine's posture during the encounter. I told him about the "Practically perfect in every way" and explained that all I got was a bit of slumped shoulders and downcast eyes. Joe demonstrated the posture back to me and said that Christine's eye position is what they called "auditory digital" in NLP which means that while I was busy yelling at her, she really didn't hear me. She was too busy yelling at herself and dressing herself down worse than I ever could or would. He told me to do something that I thought was absurd. He told me that next time she messed up, just look at her and say, "Christine, I know how hard you always try to do the right thing. Missing this assignment must be really, really upsetting for you." So, I tried it.

She collapsed sobbing into my arms and I consoled her and told her how wonderful she was and how proud I was of her always and to not worry about one small miss when 99% of all she did was stellar. Christine didn't need to be knocked down after her mistake; she'd already done that to herself. She needed to be built back up. I've never forgotten that lesson.

CHAPTER 12

Report from the Air Versus One from the Ground

Now that we have all the tools in place, let's learn some more about communication styles so that you can further refine your ability to gain rapport quickly and easily.

The difference between these two views is the next big lesson in communicating well. Some folks like to give a report from the ground. In other words, they want to tell you every bit of what their event was like in great detail as though it were happening all over again right now. Some folks like to give a view from the air. They want to tell you the gist of what went on but, from their view, details go unseen and unmentioned.

Let me give you an exaggerated example of these two types, each telling the same story, to bear this out.

The Ground View

First the ground view person. Imagine the listener asked, "How did it go with your meeting this morning?"

"Not bad but I got up around 7:00, which was not really normal for me because I usually get up at 6:45, and while you may not think 15 minutes is a big deal, minutes can add up and throw you off. I went down to make coffee but, of course, the dog was hopping up and down and needed to go out. I let him out in the backyard to relieve himself but there is a hole in the fence. I have been meaning to fix that; maybe this weekend. Anyway, I don't think he can fit through it but I worry, so I stood there and watched him and then called him in and went back to make the coffee. I went back upstairs with my cup to take a shower and get ready. I was thinking about the meeting and what would be the best way to dress. I had gone through my closet last night and picked something out but then it looked like rain when I let the dog out so I wasn't sure if that was the best outfit so I went back through to find something I'd be more comfortable in which, of course, had me worried now that I'd be late.

I left around 8:00, which I figured would be enough time since the meeting was at 9:00, and it shouldn't take more than 30 minutes to reach the meeting location. By the way have you been down Brewers Lane lately? They are putting in new water pipes or something and the road is a mess. Anyway, I got there at 8:35 and managed to get a guest parking spot that wasn't under the building but was close enough that I didn't get wet and I made the meeting with 15 minutes to spare."

Do you see the style? Report from the ground folks feel the need to give a lot of detail. They feel it is relevant in order to properly answer the question.

The Air View

Now here is the report from the air. "How did it go with your meeting this morning?"

"It was great, thanks. I was a bit concerned because I got up later than I wanted to but even with the light rain and the construction on Brewers, I managed to get there at 8:35 and find a spot near the building. I made the meeting with 15 minutes to spare."

Building Rapport with Both

Here is what you need to know about the two styles as it pertains to facilitating good rapport.

Respecting the Ground View

People who give you a view from the ground believe strongly that all of the detail is necessary in order to properly convey the story. If you are an air person you will find the amount of detail, the sheer volume of words, boring and off putting. You will likely show that feeling through words, facial expressions and body posture.

> **People who give you a view from the ground believe strongly that all of the detail is necessary in order to properly convey the story.**

Moreover, if you try to gently move them along with words, gestures or body language, they find you insulting. They will mistake your attempt to "get to the essence of the conversation" for disinterest and disrespect. They will think of you as self-absorbed, elitist and rude. They may not come out and say those things overtly but internally their brains are screaming "He's not listening! He wants me to be done. He's just waiting for his turn to talk!" Obviously this is not good for rapport.

Respecting the Air View

With a view from the air, the teller believes they have given you all that you need to know. They are not consciously deciding to redact details, their memory style is one that uses big chunks of information rather than little bits.

If you press them for more bits they get impatient with you and think you're not bright enough to follow along or are looking for ways to trip them up. They become suspicious of your motives. Their inner dialogue chides them as well. "Why do you need to know so much? Haven't I already told you everything? Do you think I'm lying about something?"

Obviously this is also not good for rapport.

> **With a view from the air, the teller believes they have given you all that you need to know. Their memory style is one that uses big chunks of information.**

Mixing Ground and Air

What about the other side of this? How does a ground listener feel when being spoken to by an air person? In a word, marginalized. Their brain is translating the view from the air like this. "You obviously don't want to talk about this with *me*. You don't think I'm important enough to share with or you think I'm too stupid to understand it all so you're throwing me the least you can to satisfy my questions and shut me up."

Do you remember the movie *Planes, Trains and Automobiles*? There is a great example of these communication styles in a conversation between the late, great John Candy and Steve Martin. Candy's character is a ground guy while Martin's is air. After telling a story in excruciating detail, Steve Martin stops John Candy with a hand held up like a traffic cop and says, "The next time you're telling a story try to have a point. It makes it better for the listener!"

This is the feeling an air person has when listening to a ground. They're bored and losing the thread. Like Joe Friday in *Dragnet*, they want to say. "Just the facts ma'am."

Adjusting for Good Rapport

So where does this leave us? Hopefully noticing these styles in ourselves and others and making respectful adjustments to facilitate our conversations.

If you're a ground view person and want to be in rapport with an air view person couldn't you make a conscious effort to editorialize less and drive to the point more quickly? There will be plenty of other times and other conversations in which you can give the details and color you want to give but for the sake of rapport, when you notice this mismatch, make the adjustment and censor yourself a bit.

Conversely, people with a view from the air can consciously slow down and offer more color commentary. You don't necessarily have to stroll through the story, but you can fill in some blanks and talk in hops instead of leaps.

There are other aspects of communication that we've spoken about that are essential to hearing and understanding the point. Things like active listening and tone and pace are about getting the point. Air view and ground view recognition is a tool for rapport. Understanding these styles in yourself and others and adjusting where it's appropriate is used to facilitate communication, deepen relationships and gain trust and respect.

A ground view person can certainly understand an explanation barked at him in clipped phrases but he will walk away wounded and be more guarded in the next conversation. An air person can certainly sit through the reading of the fine print but she will walk away shaking her head and making a mental note to avoid that "time sucker" in the future.

These should be easy reads for you if you're calibrating as I described in Chapter 11. The wounded expression of a ground viewer is easy to spot if you pause a beat to observe, after quickly offering the cliff notes to an important story. The face sags a bit, a little color may come up, the eyelids drop a tad and the outer canthus closes a little.

Just as recognizable is the bored expression of an air view person as they try to sit through, *what they believe*, is excessive detail. They may sigh, roll their eyes, tap a foot, a finger or a pencil, pick imaginary lint off of their suit, push their face forward on their neck or point a foot away from you.

A SYSTEM OF CONTEXT — CALIBRATING

Remember that when calibrating no one signal is 100% of the story. It is all a system in context. A rise in color or a change in breathing can indicate embarrassment, discomfort, anger, disbelief or fear depending on the situation. My caution is that we take it all in and allow ourselves to gut-assess it rather than pick out one or two things and try to read them verbatim.

We know about the science now. We've explored a number of tools and techniques like the importance of active listening, about being open and present, emulating tone and pace, matching and mismatching, backtracking and mirroring and mastering calibration. And we understand the two basic styles. Going forward we must practice and refine these skills to reach a level of unconscious competence, getting us to a level at which we can front-end rapport seamlessly and naturally. Developing these rapport skills is the most essential piece in the puzzle of successful business and personal relationships because when we develop rapport, we're trusted and well thought of and this is where we need to be in order to go deeper and connect authentically. It is that connection that facilitates everything else. Let's move on to cultivate some additional techniques and systems to complement our great relationships.

PART THREE

DESIRE WINS

Let me begin with Frank Fusaro's take on desire.

EXPERT TAKES

I've said this a million times, lots of people are born with the brains to be successful but only a handful of people have the heart to be successful. You have to have the heart to be a salesperson. You have to be focused. You have to be willing to take the punches.

CHAPTER 13

Born Like This?

I believe that you have everything inside of you to accomplish whatever you want to accomplish. All you need is the strategy. I know that if I ate the same foods, lifted the same weights and took the same drugs I could be as big as "The Govenator" was in his prime. It's all about the strategy.

No One Is a Natural

I do admit that there are some folks who are born with the genetic makeup to be taller or faster than others or with perfect pitch in music. I'm not saying that with the right application of training I could overcome my bodily limitations and dunk a basketball like Michael Jordan or write a sonata like Beethoven, but I feel strongly that if I immerse myself in learning and practicing anything, I will excel at whatever endeavor I choose. I don't believe that anyone I see who is crushing it in any field is simply "a natural."

I believe that there are trained and untrained bodies more than there are naturally gifted and non-gifted bodies. I believe that there are trained and untrained minds more than there are naturally intelligent and stupid people.

Let's remove the Einsteins and the Jordans from the equation for a moment since most of us reading this are not likely to be competing for a Nobel Prize in physics or MVP honors in the NBA. For the rest of us, it's about believing that we are bad at math or lack the ear to learn languages. It's the limiting belief that somehow you are gifted and I am limited.

It is true that some people take to some things more effortlessly than others but if the some people undertook massive action to improve in that same thing I believe they could equal and surpass the effortless folks.

I'm not qualified to tell you what goes in to being a natural at anything but that doesn't stop me from having an opinion. Is it biological or environmental? My bet is that environment outweighs biology. I often see that the offspring of two highly educated people are more likely to become educated themselves than the offspring of uneducated people. I see that Archie Manning's boys, Peyton and Eli, were taught to be quarterbacks from the time they entered the world and I would wager that if Michael Jordan had been adopted by the Manning family at birth, he would have been a great quarterback rather than a great basketball player.

My good friend Dr. Rob Gilbert can memorize an entire issue of *Time* magazine. Rob could not always do this. He wasn't born with a great memory. He does, however, possess a well-trained memory. Rob took memory courses and then studied and practiced the memory techniques he learned to be able to memorize an entire magazine. People will say Dr. Gilbert has a great memory but Dr. Gilbert will tell you that he has a trained memory.

I asked Debbie Kosta if great salespeople are born or made.

EXPERT TAKES

Made. We are all with heart and mind and when the heart and mind get inspired by the product and the process and you get passionate about it, you become a great salesperson.

You have to have passion. I thought I was a writer all my life.

When my mom said you're bad with numbers and you will never be a business person, I believed it because, you know, writers and artists are supposed to be bad with numbers and business. Then I went to Tony and learned I could handle numbers well; I could be a strong business person. You can't accept limiting beliefs.

Wayne Dyer was dropped off at an orphanage at 6 years old. The other kids were all crying and complaining. He reframed it into an opportunity to become self-reliant.

Developing Your Sales Gene

Joe DiGeorgi and I met when we were in our teens. We worked in a florist/gift shop in a little strip mall in Alexandria, Virginia. Joe and I were outgoing guys, easy to smile and comfortable with people coming into the store, but neither of us had any sales training.

Our boss, Mr. Street, saw we were young, fun and eager so he would challenge us to increase the amount of money in the till on those nights we worked together, sometimes offering us a few extra bucks if we exceeded the previous high total. Without the benefit of training or experience, Joe and I began to sell. For the next several months we "trained."

This was sales training 101 as we experimented with different techniques we thought of to try to get people to buy. As we developed our sales chops we began to have fun. Joe and I would test one another to see who was the better sales guy. We created our own little contests and crowned a champion on the nights we worked together. These contests amounted to some of the best training I've ever had.

We learned how to approach all types of people. We learned when to be charming and when to be serious. We learned when to speak and when to wait. We learned not to waste time on people who we judged wouldn't buy and, most importantly, we learned the twin peaks of selling. First, that in sales you have to kiss a lot of frogs before you find a prince and, second, that have to learn to like kissing frogs.

You've heard over and over that sales is a numbers game meaning that if you knock on one thousand doors you will likely find more business than if you'd knocked on ten. The reason salespeople stop knocking is rejection and lack of belief.

> **The reason salespeople stop knocking on doors is rejection and lack of belief.**

Imagine for a moment that you sell desk chairs to businesses. If you set out to canvass the 102 floors of the Empire State Building you might visit two or three floors and knock on forty or fifty doors on any particular day. But what if you learned that every business in that building was replacing desk chairs today? How many floors would you hit and how many doors would you knock now? It got like that for Joe and me and that is why I say the training was invaluable. We tested each other so often and in so many ways that we started to get good.

Joe would say, "I will bet you $1.00 that you cannot sell something to the next person who walks in." Understand that this was a gift shop filled with knick-knacks. People came in all the time to look at the little statues, vases, candles and figurines without buying.

From there the bets went to, "I will bet that you can't get that man in the blue sweater to buy something." Or, "Okay Joe, that woman in the boots is coming to the register with a candle. I bet you can't take her back to the candles and get her to buy two more." We even went as far as to challenge each other to walk out of the store and into the mall to meet someone, strike up a conversation and then invite them to come in and browse and, in the end, sell them something.

Joe and I were reading people and experiencing rejection at an excessive rate with these games but we made it fun so we learned not to take it personally. Every little bit of success we found made us chuckle and crow and added a layer of thickness to our confidence armor, allowing us to withstand even more rejection and continue to look for opportunities.

Joe and I both went on to long, fruitful careers in sales and sales management and I have to give some credit to our time at Beacon Mall and the silly games that helped us to develop our sales gene. We had, unwittingly, created a virtual immersion lab for sales training and we were the lab rats!

If you met Joe today in his job as the general manager of a big auto dealership, you might say he is a natural salesperson. Is he? I just told you about the 18 month "training" Joe and I went through. How many other parts of his life helped him to develop his sales gene?

My belief is that training wins. Hard work wins. Consistency wins. Perseverance wins. Desire wins. Greatness in sales is about the work and the learning.

It's like this with a lot of naturals. Had we been a fly on the wall for the entirety of a natural's formative years we could more fully opine about the origin of the excellence we see, but without the benefit of their history we really have no idea how they came to be who they are today. My belief is that training wins. This is classic tortoise and the hare stuff. Hard work wins. Consistency wins. Perseverance wins. Desire wins. In sales, more than in any other profession, perseverance and desire beat talent every time. Greatness in sales is about the work and the learning.

Peter Chieco had a similar training ground.

EXPERT TAKES

I grew up in the restaurant business. I learned from Mom that if you treat people right, they will come back. Just that; treat people right.

I watched my mom turn a complaint into a loyal customer by listening with respect and making sure she satisfied whatever they complained about.

In an interview with Larry Weiss he told me, "I've been selling my whole life. My home room was the home economics room so I sold the pizza and the cookies the home economics students made."

Debbie Kosta also told me about her start in sales.

EXPERT TAKES

I thought I would get some training. It was like, "Here are your leads, call them." I was a calling machine, and I fumbled and learned. I was embarrassed, and I didn't know how to ask for the business. Then, suddenly, it came to me.

I thought they will benefit from this product and, of course, you have to pay for something you will benefit from. I did get some training – he helped me with the filling out forms, the work part – but the people part I just came to on my own.

We learned a lot by listening to Tony and absorbing his philosophy. As a literature major I had read a lot. I'd hear Tony say something and think I had heard a form of it from Aristotle or Plato. Tony knows how to say things so people will understand. Tony is relevant to today. He is always learning.

Frank Fusaro believes that there are certain instincts inside of you, formed by the life you've led. He sees training as essential and that it can improve you. However, he credits desire as the biggest differentiator.

I asked him this question. "If I give you anybody of reasonable intelligence can you teach them this or do they have to have it in their belly?"

EXPERT TAKES

Look, you could make a five a seven, okay? You can manage your five to seven or mismanage a five down to a two or three for that matter, but you can't make a five into a nine.

Training and teaching are critical. However, they can only take you so far. It's the execution that's the trick. So I have to go out and recruit a seven for my business. That doesn't mean he's got to be the brightest burning church candle. He's got to have that desire, desire, desire, desire! He's got to look around at people who are successful here and say I want that; he has to be motivated.

Talent Is Not Enough

My older brother was a musical phenom. He was born with perfect pitch and, with minimal instruction, he could play just about any instrument he put his hands on. He sang really well too. Music seemed to emanate from him. So why is it that when we were 17 and 19 I was booked for singing gigs for 4 or 5 times the money he was? The sales gene.

Al was and is far better than me when it comes to music. He wrote his own tunes, sang with heart and, as I said, played a bunch of instruments. Someone could shout out a request from the audience and even if he'd never played it before, if he knew how the song went, he would mess with it for a minute or two and then play it for them. He was awesome … and broke.

When Al could have been looking at high-end venues that paid well, he was still singing in local bars. Why? Because it never occurred to him to approach a place of notoriety to try to sell himself. He wasn't stupid or lazy. In fact if someone had offered to put him in a nicer place, he'd have been excited and the crowds would have loved him. So why wasn't he playing those venues for more money? He hadn't developed his sales gene.

I sang for more money and in much nicer places because I could – and did – walk in, find the owner and get him talking. I'd find out what he was looking for, fill in the blanks for him with my band and ask for my fee. Sometimes we got there by sharing in the money he charged at the door, so I could prove the band was a draw. Sometimes we got there by relying on a referral from another club my band had played and sometimes it was just straight rapport – but we got there.

I remember one time my base player went to visit a bar we'd played a few times. The background to this is that I booked all of our gigs. I cold called the venues, got the owner's attention and did what I could to convince him that we were a good bet for the price.

My bass player could really play the bass, but he didn't have the sales gene. He came back from his visit to the bar all self-righteous about how the bar owner said he preferred to deal with him, rather than me, and how he had gotten us booked there again even though the bar was short on money. He elaborated on his story. He had booked us for about 20% less than I had been getting for us at that bar. The bar owner saw an opening to lower our price because I wasn't there and he closed our bass man for a nice discount. Of course the bar owner preferred doing business with bass man over me. He could play the bass man!

Going back to my very talented brother and me, in hindsight, if we'd had any sense, I would have become my brother's agent! He had the musical talent and I had the sales gene. The point is this. You can be the best chiropractor, the most knowledgeable real estate person, the trickiest magician, the best singer or produce the most delicious cheesecake on the planet, but unless you can get in front of the people who can use your services and convince them of how good you are, you will only be one of the pack.

You can be the best chiropractor, the most knowledgeable real estate person, the trickiest magician, the best singer or produce the most delicious cheesecake on the planet, but unless you can get in front of the people who can use your services and convince them of how good you are, you will only be one of the pack.

My dad used to say, "Cream always rises to the top" and he is somewhat right. My brother did record an awesome album and he did end up playing some wonderful venues in New York City but, my bet is that with the sales gene, not only would he have achieved all of that sooner but he would have played on big stages all over the world.

Joe, my florist buddy, and I were raised in home environments that brought out big personalities in both us; it was the nascent budding of our little sales genes. But without Mr. Street's challenges and the unintentional creation of our little sales immersion lab, we may never have fully realized the talents and developed them into lifelong, successful careers. My brother was an amazing talent but without the sales gene it was tough for him to exploit that talent to its fullest. There is no doubt that if he would have had the opportunity to learn how sales people get business (develop his sales gene), he would have played at the best jazz clubs in New York.

Finding Business

Salespeople get their business in six ways.

1. Physical canvassing
2. Telephone canvassing
3. Going deeper with existing clients
4. Networking, including family and friends
5. Referrals
6. Social media

We'll explore these methods and practices in the next few chapters.

Frank Fusaro has tried and true take on finding business. I asked him, "What do you think is the best way to find new clients? If you're advising a new business owner or a new sales guy, what do you tell them?"

EXPERT TAKES

You do your homework. You do your due diligence. You create a roster of targets – and it's got to be an endless roster, because it's going to be one after the other after the other. And then you try to get your foot in the door and get their attention in some way. You try to understand what their requirements might be. You have to sell differentiators.

I was a young CPA and I pulled out all the CPA firms. I sat with that list and, you know, again, a few minutes at a time I would pursue them. I would be persistent about getting in front of them. And I was also very active in the New York State society of CPAs. The New York State society is run by the small- to medium-sized firms mainly; the big firms don't have an interest. I met all the principles of the small- to medium-sized firms mostly, and they got to know me a little bit. And, you know, they allowed me to call on them. So, essentially, I went to where they played.

Then I made sure to sit on a committee. When you get involved in non-profits, associations, trade associations, charities, nobody wants to do anything. So if you stick your hand up and say, I'll do it, I'll volunteer, you become the kingpin.

I've watched Frank work over the past 20 plus years. He lives what he says here. He sits on several charity boards and is involved with some others. Frank is always "sticking his hand up" to volunteer. He leads with helping, but what happens in this great universe of ours? The help he gives circles right back and helps him too. Frank has met a ton of notable people through his charity efforts and those people see him as a *mensch* – a great guy – so when they need the type of services Frank offers, it is natural that they seek him out, but remember Frank's intention with every charity is to help. Frank never goes in thinking of benefits to Frank. He goes in wanting to give his talents to a worthy cause.

CHAPTER 14

The Proving Ground and Canvassing

Canvassing, both telephone and in person, is often the proving ground managers lay out for new salespeople. You've no doubt heard that sales is a numbers game. This is what they're talking about when they say that. But before we get into making contact, we need to discuss a couple of other important factors. Let's start on the surface and go deeper.

Appearance

Back in the time *Mad Men* is set, guys wore suits and starched white cotton shirts with skinny ties and wide brimmed hats and women wore dresses, pantyhose and heels. Office dress was a formal affair back in the days before Silicon Valley. Now it seems like anything goes and it is harder to navigate the multitude of fashion choices that are acceptable in the workplace.

Rule number one is to be appropriate. Don't wear shorts and a T-shirt to the boardroom or a three-piece suit to the company picnic.

Rule two is to dress slightly north of your pay grade. Unlike real estate investment, where you want to buy the ugliest house on the block, as a sales professional you want to be in "move in condition." Let other folks drift downstream to the shallow end of acceptable dress. You want to look the part of a trustworthy sales professional.

Professional and trustworthy do not equal slick. Slick, in my mind, means flashy, over the top, in your face dress. Slick fulfills one of the stereotypes the media has created for us. Slick is a suit that's too fancy or loud. It's a Rolex with a diamond bezel. Slick is garish and showy and intends that people will look at you with envy. What we want is clean, neat, subdued and classy. It may be a well cut suit, Italian loafers and a Rolex but each choice is understated, not diamond bezel, over the top.

In an office environment that is business casual, sometimes the dress code can become sloppier than the dress code that was intended. The men's standby cotton Dockers are ubiquitous in these offices but the degree of neatness from one to another can be as different as a Ritz Carlton is to a Motel 6. Both have rooms, lobbies and front desks, but they really aren't the same thing. Old, ill-fitting, wrinkled Dockers are not what was in the mind's eye of the management team when they created the dress policy yet, somehow, people too often fall to the lowest rung of what will be tolerated. *Not you!* You always want to be a cut above where you need to be. Leave the wrinkled clothes and dirty tennis shoes to the guys in the warehouse or on the loading dock. You want to be at the top rung of this ladder – neat, unstained, pressed and fresh.

Paraphernalia Counts Too

There are lots of other things that go along with appearance. Do you visit a client carrying a used yellow pad with 20 pages folded over the top or do you have a portfolio to hold your pad or a bag to carry it in? Do you have a decent pen in your hand or a blue Bic with a chewed up cap? Do you pull a creased business card out of your wallet or do you have a fresh stack to pull from?

Some of us take notes on a small laptop or tablet or even on our phones. There are a few cautions here as well. If you're using a laptop be sure the top doesn't interfere with your sightline. The "open, heart to heart" part or physical communication (see Chapter 7) can be lost with an ill placed laptop.

If you're using a phone for notes, be sure to ask permission. It lets the other person know that you're using the phone for notes, not texting as they speak. Another word about phones and notes is that at a meeting, in which you are one of several people, the same rule applies and even when you make it clear you are taking notes on your phone, be aware that others in the room will still believe you're sneaking texts or emails in during the meeting.

Calibration Revisited

Remember when we talked about calibration (see Chapter 11)? What do you think a frayed collar, wrinkled suit or chipped nail polish add up to? People calibrate instantly, taking in all of the things we went over in how to meet someone and all of these seemingly minor appearance factors. Imagine you and your competitor are running at about even going into the final selection phase on a product or service offering. Then you show up with dirty fingernails and the aforementioned half used yellow pad and chewed Bic, while she walks in dressed appropriately carrying a leather portfolio with a nice pen nestled in its leather loop. Don't you think you'd lose a bit of ground?

I have seen successful salespeople who look like fashion models and others who look like unmade beds. The successful unmade beds I've seen overcame any appearance issues with amazing rapport and sales skills. So, yes, it can be done, but why leave it to chance? There is a segment of the buying population that will not buy from "an unmade bed." There is not a section of the buying population that won't buy from you because you are neat and pressed.

I don't believe for a second that you have to look like Brad or Angelina to be successful in selling but I am certain that everything adds up in the mind of your prospect, so why add an avoidable hurdle to the process? Even if you have the mad skills I've seen in some of the unmade beds I've met in my career, your competitor may be that good too and the chewed pen cap could be the perception difference that gives her the edge.

Accept Rejection

Remember Joe and me back in Mr. Street's floral/gift shop. We experienced rejection on an astronomical scale, but that was part of the training.

Reframing rejection is an essential sales skill. If you understand that statistically you will connect 1 in 100 times then you can see the 99 rejections as a necessary part of the process.

This doesn't mean calling like a robot, believing it is all a process of odds and numbers. I have seen salespeople dialing like a computer dialing service, just throwing enough crap on the wall to see what will stick. They go from dial to dial with no compelling story or rapport hooks. They dial and dial, just getting through the required calls the manager asked them to make. NO! This is not going to work! You've got to approach each dial, each door as though these folks are definitely going to say "yes" and begin the process of utilizing your services. You have to approach each call with a state of mind that is sure they need you.

> **You've got to approach each dial, each door as though these folks are definitely going to say "yes" and begin the process of utilizing your services.**

This idea of managing your state of mind is essential. Certainly it is possible to go from door to door and dial to dial with no soul at all, and eventually someone will raise their hand and say "I'll take it." But that's like throwing a hook into the water and waiting for a fish to come by and snag itself. Fishing is better when you go where the fish are concentrated and when you have something alluring to offer. So let's go back to reframing the rejection.

Frank Fusaro told me his view on rejection in sales.

EXPERT TAKES

You know I tell people this business is not like being a professional golfer – you're on the 72nd hole of a tournament and if you make the putt you're in first place and win a million bucks but if you miss the putt you're in second place and you get $750,000. In this business if you miss the putt you get nothing.

You have to be able to deal with that. You have to be able to deal with getting an email on Sunday night, after you did a big deal and the guy is supposed to start on Monday and it says, "I'm very sorry but I never thought was going to happen … They made me a counter offer … This thing came out of the blue … My sister is in Delaware and I have to take care of her … I fell in the shower … blah, blah, blah."

That happens all the time and you have to come in and write a drop out after you already have that money counted. You've got to have some resilience to deal with that.

Canvassing

Cold Calling

Cold calling on the phone is likely the least effective tool employed by salespeople at every level of experience. It is, however, an essential tool for us all.

The salesperson who makes 100 cold telephone calls each day should find more prospects than the salesperson who makes 25 calls each day – all things being equal. This is the proving ground for a lot of sales managers. They want to see that you have the metal to bang out 100 calls a day. They want to see the desire. They want to see if you can handle the rejection and they expect a portion of new people to wash out during this process because they can't.

I asked Larry Weiss, "What's the best advice you've given to a rep on their first day on the job?"

EXPERT TAKES

The business is not what you think it is. This is not a nine-to-five business. You have to constantly be looking for business. You have to practice and learn. Selling is a profession you have to practice. You create the number of opportunities and the more opportunities you create the better you will do.

Malcolm Gladwell has the 10,000 hour rule. 10,000 hours of deliberate practice will make you world class at anything. When I started I knocked on 100 doors a day. That's like the 10,000 hours. That will make you great but nobody listens. Nobody knocks on 100 doors a day anymore, or even makes 100 quality phones calls!

Calling from a qualified list, on the other hand, increases the odds of success dramatically over calling from a generic or outdated one. I still make cold calls to introduce myself as a possible keynote speaker for various associations, companies and events. To bolster my hit rate, I buy a fresh list in a reasonable quantity. There are lots of list services out there but I prefer to bid out my list build on UpWork or Fiverr.

For those not familiar with either of these names they are networks of freelancers who perform a variety of services. I create an example of the list I want in Excel, built with column headings for each piece of information I need. Next I decide how many names I want on that list and what the geographic or other parameters should be. Then I go to the freelance network and ask for bids. I offer my spreadsheet example of the information I need, give the quantity of names I want and provide the budget I have. Freelancers who specialize in list building bid for my job and I make a selection. I then import the list into my CRM (see Chapter 15) and set up my calls.

The quality of the list and having the complete information is vital to get off to a good start. Depending on the type of selling one needs to do it may also be important to look at the website of each company and any associated news before reaching out.

Physical Canvassing

It's the same with physical canvassing. The woman who knocks on 100 doors a day will meet more potential clients than the woman who knocks on 20. Telephone and physical canvassing are like boot camp for sales fledglings. They are meant to toughen you up by setting you up for massive rejection daily.

> **Telephone and physical canvassing are like boot camp for sales fledglings.**

They're meant to teach you work ethic and desire, not a far cry from a 10-mile forced march with a 70-pound field pack strapped to your back. They're also meant to develop discipline and better people skills. Forcing yourself to get up and get at such mundane tasks each day builds the discipline you'll need to face the work you'll have to do to become a successful salesperson.

I should also mention that, for most businesses, this is the least effective of the six ways to find business. Again, that doesn't mean you shouldn't do it or that it doesn't yield results, just that the time to result ratio is less than some of the other avenues available for business development.

The Elevator Pitch

When I ran a sales team in New York City I required all new recruits to ride the elevator on their third day of work – all day. You've heard of an "elevator pitch," right?

An elevator pitch is a two- or three-sentence blurb a salesperson develops to describe what he does in a complete and, hopefully, compelling way. What I did with new recruits was to have them write their elevator pitch. Then we'd refine it together and work on presenting it well. I'd teach them all of the instant rapport strategies we went over in Part Two, reviewing body posture, facial expressions, tone and pace. Once they had it down I would have them ride the busy elevators in our building, up and down, all day.

The idea was for them to introduce themselves, with their elevator pitch, and hand a card to everyone they could. They learned to be quick and succinct because sometimes they only had one or two floors with someone and they had to present themselves in a non-offensive way and give their elevator pitch. I didn't do this to torture them; I did it for two reasons.

First, they gained great rapport and presentation skills. After doing this for a day they could meet anyone at any event and instantly gain rapport and answer the "So what do you do" question with ease and eloquence.

Second, it quelled inhibition. Salespeople have to kiss a lot of frogs; they have to push through a ton of rejection. Statistics show that something like one in one hundred cold calls ends up in a conversation and that most sales are not concluded until the fifth ask. With numbers like that, if you want to be successful, you have to be able to not just *handle* rejection but be able to swat it away like flies at a summer barbeque. You have to run through it with the understanding that it is part of the sales process.

I think it was Andrew Carnegie who said "When you dig for gold you have to remove tons of dirt first but you don't go in looking for dirt; you go in looking for gold." It's like that with selling. The conditioning I did with the new recruits helped them to see that. Door-to-door canvassing varies greatly by business type and location.

In New York City salespeople have many more restrictions than they did 20 years ago due to the intense security measures most buildings employ. But still I recommend that, depending on your level of experience and the level of security in the building, you get some cold calling done once you're inside.

At minimum the "door to the left, door to the right" method is a must. When you leave an appointment, you stop by those two doors to let those folks know about the success you're having with their neighbor and offer your services. If you're a rookie and can get away with it, once you're in the building you should knock on every door.

CHAPTER 15

Going Deeper with Existing Clients

In many sales companies there exists multiple opportunities within each client. Going deeper – mining for more business within your client base – is only made possible through rapport and attention.

Customer Relationship Managers (CRM)

If you do not use a Customer Relationship Manager (CRM) now, start using one tomorrow. It is vital to your client relationships.

Any CRM will have a host of features to help you to facilitate for your clients. Forgive me for being pedantic but I want to talk a little about CRMs from the ground up.

The essential core of the CRM is a place to store information. Basics like phone numbers, zip codes and email addresses are always at the ready and, of course, activities are scheduled, but if you use it properly it can be so much more.

When I look in my CRM to call DCC Associates, a longtime client, I see a note on my home screen that says "Marta answers the phone." Aren't I jump-starting rapport when I call DCC and say, "Good Morning, Marta. It's Frank Somma. How are things with you?" before I even ask to speak with Fred who is my contact? Haven't I added yet another bit of separation between me and my competition?

Beyond that, my CRM holds copies of any documents I choose to tack to it, like the last transaction we did together or my most recent proposal. It also keeps the thread of emails between us so that when I call I can easily reference the last conversation we had via email.

The key to any CRM is the usage. First of all, the old computer term "GIGO" (garbage in garbage out) applies here in spades. There is nothing more draining than opening up the CRM and seeing 700 activities scheduled for today because they were scheduled willy-nilly or allowed to incessantly rollover. Or going into the CRM to search for certain types of businesses and having to wade through thousands of irrelevant contacts. GIGO!

If you're smart about scheduling activities and only schedule as many calls and to-dos as you can reasonably accomplish on the day scheduled, you will be in position to adopt a rule I use for my CRM. That rule is that the week is sacrosanct; meaning I can roll over an action for a day, or even a few days, but by the end of the week, all scheduled actions for that week are completed.

Customizing Your CRM

Identifying types of companies is essential. It may be that your company has a scheme in place that categorizes businesses into sections that make sense within your company. Beyond that is the categorization I am getting at here. It's how you see your client base and more importantly how you *identify* your client base.

The technique here is similar to organizing anything from a file drawer to the files and folders in your computer to the utensils and dry goods in your kitchen. When you're ready to put something away, don't ask yourself where it goes. Instead, ask yourself, "Where would I look for this?" So what does this have to do with a CRM?

There are fields in your CRM that are open for you to interpret. Use these fields to categorize your contacts. I have contacts that I met through a certain networking group. Each of their records is tagged with the name of that group so that before a meeting I can browse through them and catch up on any business conversations I may have had with any of them since the last meeting I attended. I have client relationships in a few businesses I am involved with. I tag those clients with the appropriate business so that I can easily find them. I have also customized my CRM with fields for my "Frankie's Fabulous 14" – the 14 pieces of personal information I want to gather about my clients. I do this so that I can make a different phone call than my competitor might make.

1. Hometown
2. Hobbies
3. Marital status, spouse's name
4. Kids, grandkids, as many names and ages as possible
5. Birthday
6. Associations or clubs
7. Favorite charity
8. Movie, television and music interests
9. Vacations; when and where
10. What car does he/she drive?
11. Favorite sports teams
12. Current residence, city and state
13. College/Military Service
14. Pets

When I call Andrea, who has a new pup and a vision of working in her home office with the dog at her feet, the first thing I say is, "How is the training going? Is Molly able to sit in the office with you yet?" Then we talk about dog training and my dogs and trade some funny stories about the joys and frustrations of new puppies. Then we get around to business. I have hundreds of clients and prospects. If not for the customization of my CRM how would I remember Andrea's dog's name? How about the call to Rob when I ask how his middle son is doing in Europe while he takes a semester of college in Italy?

The big thing to remember here, as I have emphasized throughout the book, is sincerity. I am very interested in Andrea's puppy and Rob's son's adventures in Europe. This isn't a gratuitous ask. You could mistakenly deem these inquires as contrived because I keep notes in my CRM but, as I said, I have hundreds of business contacts and, let's face it, there is no way I could remember all of these important, little details without notes in my CRM.

> **You could mistakenly deem these inquires as contrived but I have hundreds of business contacts and there is no way I could remember all of these important, little details without notes in my CRM.**

From Shoe Box to CRM

In 1985 I met a guy named Bret Ashley. Bret was a partner in a computer store in Brooklyn and we hit it off instantly. I was there to sell him a copier but we also explored the idea of my company working with his to provide computer hardware add-ons for our clients. I stopped by Bret's shop from time to time to go over our business opportunities and, inevitably, we'd end up talking about fishing.

I did a good deal of fishing myself and Bret was a former freighter captain who loved tooling around in his Grady White pursuing striped bass, blue fish, sharks and tuna off the shores of Long

Island. It was the fishing that we bonded over and a great business friendship ensued.

It was during one of these visits that I happened to look over his shoulder and see a customer's contact card on the screen. Curious, I asked Bret what I was seeing on the screen. Bret introduced me to the precursor to CRMs – CMSs (Contact Management Software). He showed me a program called Goldmine and I was blown away.

Up to this point I had organized index cards in a shoe box. I had divisions for months of the year and another set of dividers for 30 days. At the beginning of a new month I would pull the cards from that month and put them into the proper days to call. CMS emulated but added a ton of functionality to this age-old sales contact system.

I was fascinated that there existed this elegant, robust, card file system on a computer! I began to research these programs. At about the same time, ACT! CMS hit the market. I may have been their first customer (lol). I remember heading to the library with my portable, 15-lb., suitcase-looking computer, the ACT! floppy discs and manual. I sat there for the entire day mesmerized by what this program could do for me.

As I think back, I credit a good deal of the success in my career to that single day in the library. I wasn't in management yet; I was a territory salesperson but with ACT! I was scheduling dozens of to do tasks, phone calls, meetings and various reminders. People in my company began to take notice. "Wow Frank, you remember everything! Wow Frank, you're on top of every detail!"

It was amazing. I sent birthday cards, remembered the names of spouses, where folks went on vacation, how many kids they had, including their names and ages, and if they had a dog or cat. I had everything I needed right in front of me. I developed Frankie's Fabulous 14; the 14 bits of information I would try to gather during conversations with business associates. I tailored my ACT! database to accommodate that information and, as I said, could bring it to the forefront with the click of a mouse.

I went on to manage a few reps, then a few teams and finally to become the VP of sales and a partner in that company. Seriously, I credit my choice to dive into that new technology, learn it well and apply it to set myself apart.

Deeper Rapport

Remember back in Chapter 6 when I talked about my wife's conversations with my business associates? I was and am amazed with the ease by which she gains rapport. She has a wonderful curiosity about people so asking these things is natural to her. She listens with rapt attention because she is tickled pink by the story of how you met or the one about your 3-year-old discovering his belly button. She leans in and asks them more questions and laughs and nods, and touches and encourages them to continue, *and* they love her.

Debbie Kosta tells me that other reps are incredulous when she tells them how she gets her biggest deals.

EXPERT TAKES

They call me and ask, "What are some of the tricks you do on sales force?" They think my secret sauce is wizardry of the sales force or some magic manipulation.

They say, "How do you get those big deals, Debbie?" And I reply, "I don't get leads; I am happy to teach you."

They don't realize – or want to realize – that I simply ask the right questions. That I probe deeper. That I begin by wanting to help.

What I am doing with Frankie's Fabulous Fourteen parked permanently and prominently in my CRM is remembering to be personal. It is too easy to make the call and go right into business matters when we're in work mode but I've found that, with very few exceptions, people prefer a friendly business conversation and that means personal.

Friendly is defined as "characteristics of or befitting a friend; showing friendship."

Friendly is defined as "characteristics of or befitting a friend; showing friendship." In virtually every case, in my experience, people prefer to do business with people they like and trust. In other words, friendly folks.

When my competitor calls Rob to ask about bidding for the services I offer or gets referred to Andrea, don't you think my conversations about the kids and the dog over the years add weight to my standing? Wouldn't you agree I am tougher to move past because I'm not just a product or service, I'm Frank? I'm Dean's grandpa who knows a little about your grandkids too. Frank, the guy who is on the board of Cooley's Anemia Foundation and contributes to your charity. Frank, the guy who runs with his dog and knows how you feel about your pets. Yes, I am a business associate but I've become more than that too.

CHAPTER 16

Networking

While writing this section of the book I was blessed with the opportunity to have lunch with two major league networkers. (The universe, once again, conspires to help.)

One of them created a networking group on his own a dozen years ago. Now it has over 50 regular members who meet monthly and lead one another into business. The other runs more than a dozen networking dinners or lunches a year. Both guys are over 60 and are still strong in business development. (That's a lesson in itself.)

Neither of them makes any profit from the networking events themselves but each puts in the time to organize and run them well. Both are very successful and neither one has to cold call for business. How about you?

Larry Weiss, who I interviewed for this book, gave me great advice when I was contemplating joining The Columbus Citizens Foundation in New York City. The Columbus Club, as it's known about town, is a comity of successful business people of Italian ancestry. The club spends a good bit of time putting positive information about Italian Americans out there and combatting the negative "Mafia" stereotype the media is so fond of. We donate to a good number of charities, giving over two million dollars in scholarship money each year to deserving young boys and girls, and put on The Columbus Day Parade in Manhattan. Joining such a prominent group appealed to my sense of duty and, as a business-man, I thought it would be awesome to have such a group to sell my wares to.

Networking groups of any kind don't work unless you do.

Larry told me this, "Networking groups of any kind don't work unless you do." He told me to volunteer for committees, show up at events and, when I did get to meet some people, look to see what I could do for them first. I am still a member of the club and I belong to Junto, a straight up, networking group. Larry's advice is spot on for both of them.

Frank Fusaro also believes in networking and in doing good works at the same time.

EXPERT TAKES

I'm involved with a few different charities. You know me from Cooley's Anemia Foundation. I was never touched by Cooley's anemia personally. Nobody in my family was ever effected by that disease but when they put that baby, Michelle, in my arms I got a little bit choked up and that was that. I was done. You know it's not a lot for me — I probably donate $10,000 a year for Cooley's — but I bring support from the Columbus Club and I've been involved with the foundation for 25-30 years. It never stops. You gave your word and you're good to see it through to the end.

Just because you're a member doesn't mean other members will throw business at you. Remember, it's all about rapport; it's all about trust. Volunteering for committees allows people to see you as you are. You get to know one another and when the need for services that one of you offers arises, the other is now inclined to bring you in. It's the same with a formal networking group like Junto. We meet monthly for a nice breakfast but it is the small group coffee meetings and lunches that allow us to really get to know each other and that's when business between us flows.

Styles of Networking Meetings

A Typical Atypical Group

The first gentleman I mentioned is Tom De Filippe. Tom offers valuation services. If you want to know what a company or a brand is worth, Tom is the guy to see. Tom's networking group is called Junto, named after Ben Franklin's own group of cohorts,[7] and is filled with top executives and business owners from various disciplines. In that way it is a typical networking group – a group of people at a common level on the business ladder.

Tom and his board are choosy about who they invite in and the result is a dynamic, interactive group who regularly invite one another to events outside of the Junto meetings. In this way, the group is atypical – it is quite exclusive and you must be invited to a meeting.

Each month the Junto members gather for a breakfast. It begins with a cup of coffee and casual conversations to catch up with each other and talk about what business opportunities one may have that could incorporate the skills of another. Tom then begins the meeting, regaling the group with a great story of a trip he took or an event he recently attended, and reviews the agenda. He introduces new members and guests with a well thought out mini-bio and why they are in attendance. He then brings up one or two members to present a deeper dive into his or her business in order for the group to gain a better understanding of what that member offers.

Tom also attends 50 or more other networking events a year. It could be a Chamber of Commerce dinner or a tax seminar but whatever it is, if Tom is there, he's meeting people, exchanging cards and then following up and getting in touch. This strategy has served him well and he has all of the business he can handle coming to him, rather than him chasing it.

MY TAKE ON NETWORKING

Networking isn't isolated to formal networking groups. There are some well-known groups you can look up and join.

Nationwide groups like BNI have multiple chapters that make it easier to find a group that has an opening for the products or services you represent. BNI and others are classic networking groups. Everyone there is there to find more business.

These groups certainly have their place but for me, joining clubs or volunteering with a charity is an oblique way to do the same thing and offers other benefits. My best advice is to do both and find what works best for you.

A Different Group Each Meeting

The same goes for Carl. Carl Gambino is a banker who creates networking dinners he calls "The Gathering." Carl finds a venue in Manhattan and negotiates a nice meal of several courses that usually costs about $65 per person. He makes zero money on the tickets. He then sends invitations out to his network of business associates who, in turn, invite other associates.

In the end, there are 50+ people meeting and chatting and exchanging contact information over a glass of wine or a cocktail as they do their meet and greet for a half hour or so before dinner. Then they pick out their dining partners for the evening and continue to meet folks and exchange ideas.

Imagine that! For the price of a dinner – that you will invariably go out for on your own – you can get the same great meal, in a really nice restaurant and ask for the contact information from a bunch of different business people who are there for the same purpose and, therefore, happy to exchange! If you were out cold calling you'd have to make 100 calls to get 1 of these high-end contacts to reluctantly talk to you. At Carl's events you can meet dozens.

This is the way business gets done. People do business with people they know, like and trust. Step one is getting to know people and these two guys have mastered the art and built their careers with it.

> ## People do business with people they know, like and trust.

In just one lunch with them I was asked to meet with an executive who needs my services and invited to four different networking events!

How many new contacts can I meet eating a sandwich at my desk or sitting on my lazy boy on Tuesday night watching *Jeopardy*?

I asked Debbie Kosta how important networking is for [Tony] Robbins Research International, Inc.

EXPERT TAKES

The hardest working person in the company is Tony. He is out there doing everything – raising money, giving money. He is always out there. He has a great presence on social media too.

Leads come in because of his networking. We did a little advertising but mostly getting the word out, being an ambassador for the product is the best sales tool. I am building an outstanding life which is what I am selling.

> Go! Go! Go! But grounded and spiritual. You have to walk
> your talk.

Family and Friends

Would you rather call someone who knows you and welcomes the
call or would you prefer to call a stranger and get hung up on?

The story of the insurance salesperson who sells to as many
family members as possible and then washes out is almost legend.
He hawks his family at summer barbeques, wakes, weddings and
retirement parties until some cantankerous uncle gets fed up and says,
"Johnny, enough with the selling and selling and selling at every
outing. If we want insurance, we'll call you!"

Family and friends is a delicate network to approach but done
properly it should be good for both of you.

I talked to Peter Chieco about networking and he had a slightly
different take on family and friends.

> ### EXPERT TAKES
>
> I don't do a lot of networking. Taking care of my clients is how I
> grow the biz. When they do well, they refer us to their family
> and friends.
>
> Once I fully appreciated that you only focus on your existing
> clients and not actively push them for referrals, the referrals started
> to flow in.

It Has to Be a Good Fit

The first order of business is that you've got to have a product and
represent a company that you really believe in. You have to believe,
with absolute certainty, that your product or service is grade A and
a good fit for your relative.

When I was selling copying machines for a small company in

NYC back in the 80s, my brothers-in-law had a nice business with a couple of dozen employees and the commensurate amount of printing and copying that goes along with a growing business. *I did not sell them copiers.*

The boys, as my brothers-in-law are referred to in my family, are exacting fellows. They do things beyond right, bordering on perfection; they never half-ass it. If they can't do a thing elegantly and be proud of the output, they won't do it. They run an amazing service organization with a die-hard loyal clientele who appreciate the lengths they go to in order to be certain that their clients are happy. The copier company I worked for was not in the same league.

We were growing fast and having difficulty keeping up with the service demands. Our clients would sometimes be down for a day or two when some of our competitors were guaranteeing 4-hour response time. We were a very sales-centric organization and did not have the focus we should have had on service. The boys trusted me. They would have been happy to give me their copier and printer business, but I never asked. I knew I did not have the service chops needed to give these two very demanding professionals the level of service they offered their clients, and expected of their vendors, so I stayed away.

When to Stay Away

We don't always work at a place we believe in completely. Some-times we sign on with a company expecting more but find out they aren't as good as we'd hoped. It is then that we need the discipline to stay away from family and friends.

I have to digress for a moment. I'm not talking about some God-awful place that you should quit the day after you started. I'm talking about a company that does not offer a product or a service that meets the standard you need it to meet for your family and friends.

It may be price. Perhaps some of your family and friends will appreciate the hell out of you if you offer Motel 6 at $50 rather than

Ritz Carlton at $500. That's fine; that's your judgment. Perhaps you are with a company that's just starting out and the service and future are uncertain. That's not the time to bring family and friends aboard.

The situation I told you about took place when I was with a small copier dealer. We gave great pricing and okay service to a lot of people, but I knew it would not be good enough for the boys regardless of price. Price was not at the top of their buying criteria; excellence was and is the standard by which they make their decisions.

I am happy to say that many years later I partnered with a long-time associate in the copier business. His company offered outstanding service. The company was and is the best I have ever seen at servicing their clients and paying attention to details. When I joined them I immediately took over the copier/printers for the boys and they have been thrilled with the change.

CHAPTER 17

Referrals

You ask for referrals all the time right? Most salespeople I ask tell me that they always ask for referrals. So why is it that, in my experience, most salespeople are rarely writing business with someone that was referred by an existing client? Because they aren't *really* asking for referrals.

Are You Really Asking for a Referral?

See if any of the scenarios below sound familiar.

Scenario I: A Weak Reach via Email

You send an email that says, "Hi Mr. Customer, I really appreciate your business; thank you. I am writing to you now as a satisfied client to ask a favor. I am trying to expand my business and I am hoping that you can send me someone you think would also like to take advantage of the same great program I offered you."

Most emails like this rarely get an answer and if they do it is a vague promise to "look around for you" or to "keep you in mind."

Scenario II: A Weak Reach via the Phone

YOU: Hi Mr. Customer. I hope all is well with our service so far. I'm calling because I was wondering if you can help me out. Do you know another business who would like to take advantage of the same great savings I offered you?

CLIENT: I'm right in the middle of something. Let me think about that and get back to you.

Scenario III: A Gallant (but Fruitless) Attempt in Person

YOU: Hey, Mr. Customer. I'm glad you're happy with our service. I'm trying to expand my business. Do you have any business associates I can reach out to?

CLIENT: Yes, I probably do. Let me think about who and shoot you an email.

YOU: That would be great. Thank you!

I have seen all three of these scenes played out, literally, hundreds of times without producing a viable lead. Why not? The ask seems okay. You're not being a PITA. You're talking to a (presumably) happy client. Why wouldn't they just offer you up their contact list?

There are a few reasons why not. One is that it is difficult to think of someone on the spot when your brain isn't there. In other words, you are asking the client to do some complex math without having eased them into math mode. To think about you, what you offer, how they feel about it, what its usefulness is, who else may find it useful, if that person is in a position to afford it, and if they want to expose themselves by giving you a name is a lengthy equation.

Another reason might be that they earnestly would like to help you but once they leave your company, or the phone call, the memory of your ask gets back-burnered and continues to slide down the priority list all the way to the non-urgent, non-important quadrant and is eventually forgotten.

It may also be that you aren't in the rapport you think you are. You need to check the situation and calibrate further as you were taught in Chapter 11. Is their smile authentic? Does it reach their eyes? Are they aligned with you physically when you're talking or is there a sense that they need to move on from the conversation?

The Law of Reciprocity

Let me ask you this question. What is the best way to hear a new joke? Tell someone else a joke. The minute you tell someone a joke they begin to go through their own mental "joke inventory" to come up with a joke to tell you. Keeping that in mind, what's the best way to get a referral?

You don't even necessarily have to have a referral right there in hand. If you broach the subject you will put yourself in a much more likely position to receive a referral. Let's chart this conversation.

Scenario IA: Via Email

YOU: Hi, Ms. Customer. I am reaching out today because I was really impressed with your business. I belong to a few networking groups and would like to be able to suggest your company when the need for widgets arises. Do you have some materials you can send my way?

CLIENT: Wow, that's awesome Gina. I will email you a few things. I don't have a formal compensation plan for outside referrals but I'm sure I can figure out a way to compensate you.

YOU: That's very nice of you but rather than compensation, I'd like to come by and meet for 15 minutes. We can open up our contact lists and see who we have that may be a fit for one another.

Zig Ziglar said, "You can have anything you want in life if you just help enough other people get what they want."

The law of reciprocity is real. In his great book about happiness,[8] Martin Seligman described an experiment he used to prove this law.

He invited people to come to the psychology building to participate in an experiment. What they didn't know was that the experiment was taking place in the waiting area right after they arrived.

An applicant (Jess) would enter to find another individual sitting in the waiting area for their appointment. The person already seated was actually a staff member (Joe). They'd introduce themselves and after a minute or so of small talk, Joe would tell Jess that he was selling raffle tickets for his church. Then he'd ask Jess to buy a raffle ticket. Those attempts were successful only about 20% of the time.

The other scenario was similar but the law of reciprocity was introduced. The staff member (Joe) again would be sitting in the waiting room posing as another applicant. When the subject (Jess) arrived, they'd introduce themselves. This time, after a minute of small talk, Joe would say, "Excuse me a moment. I am going to get something to drink." Then he would disappear for a moment and return with two cans of soda saying, "I was at the machine grabbing a soda and thought you might like one too," and hand the soda to Jess. Again, after a minute of small talk he'd introduce the subject of his church raffle and asked if Jess to buy a ticket. After getting the can of soda, the applicants bought a raffle ticket 100% of the time.

The power of reciprocity is undeniable. When you approach your clients with something to give, human nature writes the rest of the script.

The power of reciprocity is undeniable. When you approach your clients with something to give, like in the above conversation I laid out where our salesperson, Gina, offered to pitch her client's products at her networking meeting, human nature writes the rest of the script.

Selective Attention

Another great way to get referral business is through the law of selective attention that I described in the very beginning of the book (see Chapter 1). Do you remember Mark, my rapid dial accountant? Mark is combining two laws in one call.

Just by calling, by inserting himself into the psyche of his client, Mark is positioning himself for the law of selective attention. For the next little while following Mark's call that client will have his antennae up (subconsciously) for accounting situations Mark is suited for even though Mark never asked for a referral during his call.

The other law at play when Mark calls is reciprocity. Mark is calling his contact list asking how they are and if they need anything. He is offering to help which, of course, prompts them to think about and ask how they can help him.

Leading to Referral

There is also a way to straight out ask for a referral that is far better than the typical examples I laid out earlier in this chapter – we lead our client to the referral.

Do you remember watching courtroom drama shows on television? In almost every one of them there comes a point during the questioning of a witness, when the opposing counsel jumps up and says, "Objection your honor! Counsel is leading the witness."

Understand what's happening in that moment. It means that the attorney is using a form of questioning that is so powerful that it is against the law! Leading questions prompt people to give you the information you are leading them to. A leading question is presented as a statement of fact that the asker is requesting the responder confirm. In a lawsuit leading someone to draw a particular conclusion is unfair and therefore disallowed; in sales it is one of the tools great communicators use to help people get unstuck.

Once again, here is the typical referral interaction.

> **YOU:** Hi, Mr. Customer. I hope all is well with our service so far. I'm calling because I was wondering if you can help me out. Do you know another business who would like to take advantage of the same great savings I offered you?
>
> **CLIENT:** I'm right in the middle of something. Let me think about that and get back to you.

Next time, try this. After the initial pleasantries, go into your referral ask by opening up your client's brain and leading him to the referrals.

> **YOU:** John, you've been a VP in the insurance business for quite a while now, haven't you?
>
> **JOHN:** A bit over 20 years now I guess.
>
> **YOU:** Wow, 2 decades! During that time I'd imagine you've met a bunch of other insurance executives, right?

So what's happened so far? You have established a foundation. John has been an insurance executive for over 20 years. In the questions that follow, that foundation will disallow John from denying some of your assumptions.

With question two, you have positioned John's brain to focus on executives he knows in the insurance industry. John cannot even answer your question without bringing up the image of one or two other insurance executives, can he? If he doesn't want to give you a name, he still needs to conjure up the image of the person whose name he doesn't want to give to you. Even if you ask John not to think of another executive in the insurance business, he has to think of one in order to identify who not to think about. Get it?

Okay, try this. Right now, *do not* think of a white tiger roaring. You've got to picture the white tiger roaring in order to know what *not* to think of!

You have also helped to lead him to the information you're hoping to get by adding the word "right" at the end of a sentence. There is something about adding that affirmative assumption at the end of a sentence that makes it impossible for John to say, "No, I haven't met any other executives in the insurance industry." You are asking a leading question. The answer is already known by both of you so he has to confirm it. Not verifying it would be weird and obviously false.

If you've followed along up to this point then you're in rapport with John when you ask the leading question. Remember, again, a leading question is one that we both know the answer to. When you ask a leading question you aren't so much asking as prompting.

With that question asked and the affirmative assumption tacked on the end, John is literally going through his mental rolodex and identifying insurance executives he knows. This is akin to opening up Chrome and googling insurance executives but, instead, your googling insurance executives in a different browser – John's brain.

Your next move is to ask another leading question with another affirmative assumption tacked on. This will bring John closer to offering you those names he has cued up in his frontal cortex right now. With the google search over, and the images of a few of his contemporaries parked in the front of his mind, the interaction continues.

> **JOHN:** Yes, I suppose I have.
>
> **YOU:** So, knowing so many of these folks over the years, if I asked you to, you could probably name a few off the top of your head right? (Wait for and watch John either nod or signal verbally that, yes he can.) What I'd like to do is grab a pen and just jot down two or three. That works, yes?

Okay let's chalkboard this section. Your first reply is a confirmation of an assumed truth – John knows a lot of other executives.

The formation of your next question is interesting.

You say "If I asked you to" and "you could probably." The nuance here lies in the "If" and the "probably." It may seem very subtle to you but the softening of the ask with these two words is what makes this request work. John knows you want the names but his brain is hearing a hypothetical question that is easier to quickly agree with and he will nod or speak his agreement.

Your next remark, "What I'd like to do is grab a pen" is different from "I will grab." Again, subtle but effective. "What I'd like to do is grab a pen and write down two or three" is getting tacit permission. You aren't telling John you're getting a pen and he'd better be ready to sing! You're offering him a chance to say "No, I don't want to give you names to jot down." You're asking, yet, assuming permission. Get it?

Make this referral script your own. Use your language and pose the questions in a way that works congruently with who you are. Just remember the nuances, affirmative assumptions and imbedded commands that are baked in.

When leading to referral, remember the nuances, affirmative assumptions and imbedded commands that are baked in.

CHAPTER 18

Social Media

In this chapter I'm supposed to tell you how to use social media to sell and then give you an awesome story about how my old navy buddy was connected on Facebook to the purchaser of a major company and, through that connection, I did a ten million dollar deal.

Sorry, that didn't happen. I don't have one of those wonderful, serendipitous stories to tell.

A Yellow Flag Moment

What I will do is put up the caution flag here. People look you up. It may be on LinkedIn or Facebook or Twitter or they may just google you, but proceed along your social media path with this knowledge firmly implanted.

An inappropriate rant on Twitter or a compromising picture of you on Facebook could cost you dearly. I remember interviewing a lovely young woman for a receptionist job. She was polite, well–dressed, articulate and presented herself extremely well. Her profile picture on Facebook was one of her, dressed in a skimpy outfit, with some radical tattoos in view, holding a nine-millimeter pistol and pointing at the camera with a rather menacing look on her face. I know a lot of you are questioning me for commenting about the skimpiness of the outfit, or her choice of tattoos, and her right to own and display a gun. You've got a point, and while, as an armed forces veteran, I feel very strongly about our personal freedoms and I would fight to the death to defend her right to show herself in this way, it gave me pause to hire her.

Be cautious about what you put out there.

LinkedIn, Facebook and Instagram

In terms of business from social media there are a lot of components. I am certainly no expert. In fact, I'm a novice in this area, but I am happy to share my experience, and perhaps whet your appetite a bit in this area if it isn't a place you've been comfortable to explore so far.

LinkedIn

LinkedIn is the accepted platform for business. While you do see birthdays announced and some personal information on display there, the accepted behaviors seem to be that personal things, like the cool restaurant you went to or pictures of your new grandchild, are the domain of Facebook while your promotion, new job, business acquisition, new hire or new product, belong on LinkedIn. Because of this there are a few basic rules I would follow on LinkedIn.

First, your profile picture ought to be indicative of the way you dress at work. While you may look awesome in the pic at the tiki bar with a Hawaiian shirt and Panama hat, holding up a coconut with an umbrella and a straw in it, it isn't a proper photo for your LinkedIn profile.

Under your name and photo, there should be a succinct description of what you do. Under my name, for example, it says, Sales Expert and Speaker. Beyond that, you ought to have your company website and a good description of the services you offer.

LinkedIn is also great for sending messages to folks you want to meet. You can see who you may have in common, connection-wise, and reference that in your ask. You can also reach out to friends who are connected to people you want to meet and ask them to make an introduction for you.

Additionally, when I am approaching someone for business, I always look them up on LinkedIn for some additional information and to see if I can find a connection we share.

Facebook

I have a personal page on Facebook and a business page as well.

I use the business page for a variety of things like posting a video each week to introduce and point people to my weekly blog post. If I am doing a live event, I advertise it here as well. You'll notice that Facebook sometimes prompts you to boost a post. Boosted posts are the most basic advertising option Facebook has to offer. Facebook has reduced the organic reach of posts, which means that a post, by itself, will not likely reach many of the people you would consider your target audience. With boosted posts, Facebook takes a previously shared post from your Facebook business page and makes it more prominent across the platform. I have been schooled by folks with more experience that there is very little to be gained with boosted posts. Instead, I post ads on Facebook. In my limited experience, the ads have worked. I even booked a speaking gig, having nothing to do with the ad, because it was seen by someone who happened to be looking for a speaker like me for an upcoming event.

As I said, I do not boost posts but it is true that with each of these boosted posts or news feed ads Facebook allows you to outline the demographic and set a budget. I have a wonderful person, Addison Sargisoff, who manages social media for me. After walking through an ad with her to select the audience and reach and set a budget, I am confident that I could do it on my own if I had to. Addison does it so much better and more often than me that it could just be she makes it look easy, but I suggest that if you don't have an Addison you can point and click your way to launching your first ad without a ton of difficulty.

Instagram

Instagram seems to straddle the two. It feels more personal but many businesses use it. Because of the format, using pictures and limited amounts of text and links, it's not optimized for business but great business messages can be posted there in an artistic sort of way. With the fairly recent introduction of Facebook Stories (a direct challenge to Instagram), it will be interesting to see what prevails. For our purposes, it's great to have a presence on all three and often you can repurpose part of a LinkedIn or Facebook post for Instagram and post a picture, description and the link that points to these stories on Twitter.

My experience with all of these is this – Tweet or get off the pot. Being active on social media, meaning that you post content on a regular basis, is imperative if you plan to use them for any sort of ask. It doesn't take a lot of effort. There are services, like Hootsuite, that allow you to easily manage content across platforms. You don't have to camp on social media. You're a sales professional but if you have professional pages on any of these platforms, you do need to be sure that you have a regular presence.

> **The basic formula for all social platforms is to give more than you get and to treat it as you would a live social encounter.**

The basic formula for all of these social platforms is to give more than you get and to treat it as you would a live social encounter. By that I mean don't "show up and throw up." I get friend requests and invitations to connect from people who are in the periphery of my business. That is, they make money from doing business with people like me. I used to say yes easily to all those requests but now the "show up and throw up" crowd has me acting a bit more cautiously.

By "show up and throw up" (an elegant phrase I learned from my coach, the great, Jane Atkinson of speakerlauncher.com) I refer to the people who ask you to connect and 3 minutes after you accept, you're hit with a barrage of information, requests or product and service offerings. If you met me at a local chamber meeting would you pitch me on your services right after the handshake? No, you wouldn't, so don't do it on the social platforms either. In any and all situations you've got to earn the right to proceed in certain directions.

When I asked Frank Fusaro about bringing in business I was surprised to hear him mention social media. First of all, Frank is a networking machine in person. He attends a board meeting, a charity event, a dinner or a networking event many evenings each week. Second, Frank is about 70 years old and we don't commonly associate people of his generation with social media. And finally, the guy has arrived. He is wonderfully successful. He has a world-class company that's doing very well. Yet, here is what he said when I asked him what made him good at bringing in business.

EXPERT TAKES

It starts with the basics of opening the door, getting in front of a person and learning how to relate to them. You walk into an office and look around, right? The guy's a golfer, the guy went to St. John's, the guy did this or the guy did that, the guy's got six kids or whatever.

Today, you do a LinkedIn search before you even get there. I never go visit the person without looking at LinkedIn first and finding out something about them – where they went to school where they grew up, what company they started at, etc.

You start out with them being impressed that you spent time learning about them and the company. You find the common ground to begin to relate to a person and continue to ask questions, learning to understand their needs and requirements so you can fulfill them. You don't go and call on somebody in a bank without looking up them and the bank first.

I interviewed a guy for 5 minutes this morning he said, "How many people do you have?" I said about a hundred or something like that. He said, "Oh, what areas are you in?" What the hell? You're seeing me about a job in my company and you don't look at the website? You don't know the areas that we have? You don't know anything about us? You didn't even spend 5 minutes on our website?

CHAPTER 19

Negotiating

Now that we have some rapport building skills under our belts and we can employ some techniques for getting business, let's talk about practical uses of some of these skills.

Negotiation is a scary word to a lot of people. Maybe because it is so overplayed in the news with stories of big contract negotiations. We hear about unions and owners staying up all night to conduct "around the clock" negotiations or congress meeting for days at a time to negotiate over a bill with each side digging in their heels and giving no ground until they are faced with a government shutdown. When they finally take a break, some weary looking guy with a 2-day beard has a microphone thrust into his face and offers a comment – really it's a well-crafted soundbite meant to look like a comment but the purpose is more for PR outside of the negotiating room than to help the process inside of the room.

It's unlikely that you are reading *B2B Is Really P2P* and trying to learn the skills to avoid a government shutdown or to give the New York City teachers union better benefits. However, we are involved in negotiations all the time and I want to share with you just two rules to apply, along with the skills we've learned already. These two rules have helped me tremendously in thousands of negotiations whether I am selling a product, buying a product or hiring a service.

1. There is no giving without getting.
2. Every giveback is a bloodletting.

Let's dig into both of these rules.

No Giving Without Getting

There is no giving without getting means that each exchange in a negotiation should be reciprocal. This isn't to say that we get something tangible back like money, features or services with each exchange, but rather that we further our own cause with each exchange.

For example, if I am a contractor offering to install a new bathroom and my client asks me for a more aggressive price I can agree to the concession if:

- I get a larger deposit,
- I get a deposit today,
- I can accelerate your payment process,
- You take care of the final painting or
- You order the dumpster.

You get the idea I think, but let me give you the tried and true way I make these counter offers.

Remember this phrase. "If I, will you?" I have drilled "If I, will you?" into the heads of thousands of salespeople. This little phrase aids in both of my rules of negotiating. It helps to show value to what you're giving up and builds in the reciprocity rule of there is no giving without getting.

"If I, will you?" This phrase shows value and builds in the reciprocity rule.

Let's go back to the contractor putting in a new bath. When the homeowner makes an offer that is less than the asking price, the contractor should lead with, "Wow, that is a significant discount. I'm not sure if I can do the bathroom for that price. *But if I* can get close to that number, *will you* be able to give me a deposit today? *Will you* take over the ordering of the dumpster we'll need? *Will you* do a deposit today and 50% of the balance after we do the demo?

You get the idea here. *If I, will you* allows you to give in a bit in return for either conveniences, firm closes or real money concessions. It also sets the table for rule number two: every giveback is a bloodletting.

Every Giveback Is a Bloodletting

When I was a kid, growing up in New York, my dad was a beer and soda man. This was back in the 1960s when the milkman climbed the steps to your porch and put glass bottles of milk into a metal box and "the Sharpie" rode slowly up and down residential streets ringing a bell so folks knew to bring their knives for sharpening. The fruit man took that same slow route with an open truck filed with fresh fruits and vegetables and my dad's job was to drive his truck filled with cases of beer and soda and carry them into all of the homes on his route. In addition to the regular deliveries, Dad would sometimes have to deliver kegs of beer to homeowners who were having a big backyard bash. It was during those keg deliveries that I learned rule number two for negotiation.

In 1965 tapping a keg of beer took a skilled hand. If you broke the seal at the top of the keg without the tap being seated properly and firmly in place, the keg would lose its pressure and go flat. The tapping mechanism was a complicated handful of metal with a threaded end, bulky hand wheel and pump. When we kids were off from school Dad would sometimes take one of us to work with him. On this particular Saturday I was the chosen one and rule number two was burned into my brain.

It was late June and there must have been a bunch of graduation parties and backyard weddings because on the day I rode along my dad had to deliver about a half dozen kegs. When we got to the first stop Dad hoisted the keg on to his shoulder and I carried the heavy, complicated tapping device. Dad's job was to deliver the keg, not to set it up and tap it. I imagine his boss didn't want the liability if the tapping went poorly and the keg got skunked.

Dad set the keg down in a metal washtub filled with ice, took the tapping gear from me, handed it to the customer and presented the bill. The guy looked at the weighty tap in his hand, then at the top of the keg and said to Dad, "Do you know how this works? Would you start the tap for me?"

Dad replied, "I've seen it done and I have done some but I'm not 100% sure of it."

The guy said, "Well, I have no idea how it works. Would you give it a try?"

Dad looked very unsure of himself as he took the tap from the customer. He turned it over in his hands a few times looking at the handle and the thread. He held it to the top of the keg seating it this way and that for a few seconds and then looked at the customer and said, "I'm no expert but I'm pretty sure this is how it goes. I could give it a shot if you'd like."

The customer gave Dad the green light and he focused like he was doing microsurgery. He hesitated for a moment, checking that all was lined up and then he pressed it down and turned the handle. We heard the hollow "thunk" as the seal broke. There was no hissing and no beer spraying about and that, coupled with the "thunk," let me know Dad had tapped the keg perfectly. Dad wiped his brow in relief, as the customer let out his breath, and dug in his pocket, smiled and tipped Dad a dollar.

During the next two keg deliveries a similar scene played out.

The customer would look at the complicated tapping gear and turn to my dad with a helpless look asking him to tap the keg for him. Again Dad would put out the disclaimer that he was no expert but had done it a handful of times. Then he would turn the tapping mechanism around in his hands again, studying it and gingerly place it on top of the keg. Again he focused like he was doing microsurgery and again we heard that hollow "thunk" as he expertly tapped another keg.

When we got back into the truck after about the fourth such tapping my brain was spinning. Is my dad okay? Is he losing his memory? Why is it so hard to do each time? I felt like I could even do it now after having seen him do it four times. I turned to him with concern on my face. I said "Dad, how come you don't know how to do the tap yet? How come you keep forgetting and struggling to figure it out every time?" He put the truck back in neutral and turned to face me with a wry smile.

He said, "Frankie, I've tapped dozens of kegs and I could do it in 2 seconds if I wanted to. But if I do, the guy is going to tip me 50 cents or maybe not at all. If I struggle a bit and take my time, I usually get a buck; sometimes two because it looked harder to do. Remember this, Cheech, people don't pay for easy. *People don't pay for easy.*"

**"Remember this, Cheech," my dad said.
"People don't pay for easy.
People don't pay for easy."**

That's where rule number two first began to emerge in my consciousness – "Every giveback is a bloodletting." What my little 8-year-old brain learned that day is the concept of value. This is why rule number two matters. If someone asks for a concession and it is instantly granted, how do you think they feel about the value of what they were just given? Not much is the answer. Anything too easily given lacks value in the eyes of the receiver.

Value Is in the Eye of the Beholder

In my live sales seminars I often do a mock car sale. I pick two members of the audience to participate. I tell them that I have a used car for sale and I am asking $10,000 and they will each, separately, try to buy it. They are allowed to make up any story they want to negotiate the price. They can point out a dent or say the tires need to be replaced soon or that there is a rip in the upholstery. I send one person out of the room and begin the sale with the other.

She offers me $8,000, saying that the bumper has rust on it and the tires look old. I come down to $9,500, telling her how I changed the oil every 3,000 miles and tuned the car up every fall. She tells me her neighbor has a similar sedan, only slightly older, and is asking only $8,500 and then offers me that sum. I tell her a guy called me on the phone and sounded like he was willing to pay full price and maybe I should hold off until he can get here tomorrow. We go back and forth a few more times and finally I say, *if I* am willing to go below $9,000, *can we* conclude this now? We settle on a sale price of $8,850.

I ask her if she thinks she got a good deal and she responds, "Yes, I think I got the price down to the lowest you would go and it is over $1,000 less than the asking price." Both rules of negotiation were at play here. I got with every give by getting her to increase her offer beyond what she had on the table, and I kept the increments I was willing to discount very small because every giveback has to be a bloodletting.

I then bring the second buyer in from outside of the room. He has no idea about our back and forth negotiation. He doesn't know we settled at $8,850.

I begin the mock sale again telling him my asking price is $10,000. He offers me $7,500. I shout "SOLD!"

Then I ask him if he thinks he got a good deal. He invariably tells me, "No, he does not think he got a good deal. He thinks he should have offered less." The difference here is obvious isn't it? The second bidder got a much better deal than the first, yet the first felt that she got a good deal and the second guy did not. *Value. Value. Value.*

In the first negotiation I held on to my price. Each concession was small, letting my buyer's subconscious know that I valued each dollar I was letting go of and that they would not come easily – a bloodletting. The perceived value of the car was higher because of my attitude in the negotiation. If I'd just rolled over at the first ask, what would my buyer think the real value of my car was? In the end I also incorporated my "If I, will you" when I asked "If I can go below $9,000 can we finish this now?"

With the second buyer I broke both of my rules. I gave without getting and did not infuse any value. I gave it away like penny candy. I showed no pain; I didn't try to hold on to any of it. In other words, *it was valueless to me.*

I exhibited how little value that $2,500 held when I gave it away without a thought. I told my buyer that the vehicle was, in fact, worth far less than $7,500 and I was happy to beat him by taking that price. This isn't philanthropy; it isn't charity work. I'm not selling my car to my kid and lopping of most of its value because it is a gift. This is a business transaction and in a business transaction everything you give or get has value assigned to it. Sometimes that value is obvious, like when I see a sport coat in Macy's for $250, but when there is a negotiation the value is often determined by the attitude of the negotiators.

"Want" at Odds with "Vulnerability"

Another important thing to remember when negotiating a sale is this, the one who wants the deal the most is also most vulnerable to a bad price-to-value equation.

If you really, really want that candy apple red, vintage Corvette you are likely to stretch your value proposition as far as you need to in order to get it. You may know logically that the value of the car is between $15,000 and $18,000 and you may have intended to be closer to 15 than 18, but if the seller is holding firm at $18,000 and you really love the car, you will find a way to justify paying for it.

At the same time, if you look at it as though you don't love the car; if you have an "I could take or leave it" attitude, and the seller needs the deal, then the opposite is true. The seller enters the negotiation believing he will sell closer to the 18K price but the buyer's indifference causes him to offer a lower price as an incentive to get the buyer to bite. It is like this in every negotiation there is. The one who wants the item or outcome more or who wants the process to end more quickly is always vulnerable to getting the short end of the stick.

Fear of Loss Rules

Another very important thing to know about any negotiation is that fear of loss is the strongest motivator there is. Promise of gain is nice, but fear of loss rules.

> **Promise of gain is nice,**
> **but fear of loss rules.**

I buy my airline ticket to travel to Florida in January because the promise of warmer weather than I have in the northeast has motivated me to buy. However, if I am hemming and hawing about buying that ticket and then find out there is only one seat left on the flight, I am suddenly more motivated to act now. The fear that I will lose the only seat left will get me off the fence one way or the other.

This is a tried and true method to get folks to act. I may have been thinking about new living room furniture for a month or two and even done some shopping but a 1-day sale, with an authentic 50% discount, will get me off my old lazy boy and into the store with my credit card leading the way

Please notice that I said "an authentic 50% discount." Don't give someone a deadline that isn't really a deadline. Don't tell me the price is for "this month only" or that you only have one left at the lower price unless it's true.

You don't do this for the first and most obvious reason. It's wrong. It's dishonest. It fulfills the stereotype I railed about in Chapter 1. If you are on a month-to-month sales quota it is very tempting to use this ploy when it isn't real, but it's just plain wrong. If you have pricing authority, meaning you have room to move on the price you propose to your client, and you offer a discount that ends, you'd better be willing to jack that price back up and lose the deal if the client doesn't bite on your offer.

To come back the following month with some convoluted story of offering the same discount chips away at your integrity.

Aim for a Win-Win Outcome

My final piece of negotiation advice is to think about this as a cooperative. It may seem counterintuitive to consider the other person. After all, you want your part of the deal to go your way, right? Let me tell you a story.

In the early 2000s we decided to put an extension on our home and add a large kitchen and master bedroom. We live in an antique home that was built in the early 1800s and most of the rooms are small and without much closet space. We are in a nice town with some large expensive homes around us and felt that giving our antique home some modern conveniences would help us to keep pace with the rising values in the area.

At the time I was in my 40s and at the height of my sales career. Our company was growing by leaps and bounds and my sales teams were absolutely on fire. We were crushing the numbers and the sales managers and I all felt like we could negotiate a nuclear arms deal with Iran while drinking a latte and getting a manicure. We were a very confident group in a very sales-centric company. I tell you all of this because what I did in this construction negotiation has a lot to do with where I was coming from at that time.

I thought about the project and the construction companies and deliberately decided to interview contractors in the dead of winter. My thought was that winter is a time when contractors have no money coming in so I would use that to my advantage and get a better price. I could see each one of them willing to drop a little further than they hoped to because I was ready to write a big deposit check as soon as they did and they'd have income during a time when they usually had none.

I knew I was a sound negotiator and planned to bring all of my skills to bear because this was a big deal for me. I estimated the job to come in at over $150K so even 10% off was a lot of money.

I had interviewed a couple of contractors and had a good sense of where the job should come in. The final guy was who I thought I would end up with because of the way he came to me. Alan had been recommended to me by my good friend, Rick. Alan was a nice guy and definitely knew his business. He had done an addition for Rick and done it well. Rick is a good negotiator himself and a very detail-oriented guy so I felt that if Alan got a thumbs up from Rick, he must be good and his price is probably reasonable.

Alan came in and bid for the job. Then, I kicked his ass.

The combination of his winter need and my win-at-all-costs mindset got him to take almost 30% less than his asking price. I was very pleased with myself. I bragged about it to my wife. I bragged about it to my kids. I bragged about it to my mom and dad.

When I got to work and had my managers in for a meeting, I

opened the meeting with an account of how masterfully I had nego-
tiated this deal saving myself tens of thousands of dollars. There
were high fives and back slaps and all of the hard-edged humor that
our sales culture had spawned to crow about victories like this.

The entire project was to take 3 to 4 months. It went on for well
over a year! (Pride goeth before the fall!)

What happened was that Mr. Negotiator, me, had driven the
price so low that the contractor wound up doing a lot of the work
himself. He couldn't afford skilled labor! There was no money to
pay people. There were arguments and threats as I tried to get him
to show up and finish the job. It was agonizing for Deborah and me
as we looked around at our incomplete home but couldn't really
do anything about it.

I thought, "I know, I'll hire someone else to finish and then I'll
sue the bastard!" But I got cold feet. What if I spent a bunch of
money with someone else to finish and then didn't recoup it in a
lawsuit? How could I negotiate a good price with the next guy
when I was obviously in dire need? I was speaking with my brother-
in-law, Pete, about the situation and when he gave me the answer,
I nearly had a heart attack. He said, "Offer the guy more money
to finish."

To many of you reading this Pete's suggestion may not be the
bolt of lightning it was to me. It may even seem obvious, but this
flew in the face of my very existence, my persona, if you will. I am
a negotiator and you, Mr. non-sales guy, are suggesting I give back
some of my hard-earned winnings? That's exactly how I'd thought
about it. I won and the contractor lost. It was a contest and I bested
him. I struggled to see Pete's point. You see, when you're a hammer,
everything looks like a nail. (Contracting pun intended.)

I have a ton of respect for my brother-in-law Pete. In fact, I
think he is among the smartest and most capable people I have ever
met, so I took what he said to heart and really thought about it.
I was responsible for where I was. I had driven the price into the

dirt. I had contrived to bring the contractor in when I knew he'd be most vulnerable to a strong negotiation and I had brought all of my skills to bear to get a fantastic price. Winner, winner, chicken dinner ... *Not!*

This was a classic lose-lose negotiation. Alan didn't get the money he wanted and I didn't get the job I wanted. So where is the big win?

I took Pete's advice and offered more money and tied it to mile markers to be sure we made the progress we needed to, in the time we needed to. I wish I could say that the contractor and I went off into the sunset and developed a beautiful friendship but that isn't the case. The damage of my intense negotiation and his subsequent lack of performance was too much to overcome. The job got done, and I love it, but that is where the story ends.

This was a huge lesson for me in negotiation. Up to this point in my life, sadly, win-win had never occurred to me. Negotiation was like arm wrestling for me. If I was strong enough, I could bend you backward and win.

Roger Fisher is the Harvard law professor who revolutionized negotiating. Fisher wrote the best-selling book, *Getting to Yes* and is credited with the idea of "win-win."[9] Subsequent to Fisher's book Stephen Covey wrote one of the most widely read business books of all time, *The 7 Habits of Highly Effective People.*[10]

Habit 4 is Think Win-Win. Covey said:

> Most people have been scripted in the Win-Lose mentality since birth. The ONLY way to truly influence others is to adopt a frame of mind and heart that constantly seeks mutual benefit in all human interactions.

Suffice it to say that I was a day late and a dollar short on this wonderful strategy. But now that I've learned it, I won't make that mistake again!

This is by no means meant to be a complete treatise on negotiation. There are volumes written on the subject and courses offered all over the world but these few points, in the world of selling, convincing and persuading have helped me tremendously.

CHAPTER 20

Sales Is Fiercely Personal

Sales gurus will tell you not to take it personally. I understand that. It means that I should see the rejection as a rejection of my services and not a rejection of Frank Somma. My problem with this advice is *that it is personal*.

The art of selling, at its best, is intensely personal.

I understand the pundits and their need to advise me to separate me from my professional offering, but I can't. I *am* my professional offering! When I approach a call or a new contact, I am doing all I can to reveal as much of myself as possible because I am better than the average bear. Because I, Frank Somma, will make the difference in whatever commoditized product I am offering and the more of me the client gets to see, the better my chances of getting the business is.

My Reframes

Let's face it. Today my client can practically point and click to buy a luxury yacht! If I want them to do business with me, then *me* has to be the first differentiator.

If I want clients to do business with me,
then me has to be the first differentiator.
I am my professional offering!

Rescue from the Less Capable

This is my reframe in approaching every contact, every door, every dial, every introduction – I want to save that person from doing business with someone less capable than me. I want to rescue them from the sea of less-than-honest business people out there looking to take advantage of them or, if not to take advantage, at least to press their own advantage and take what they can get away with. I even want to save them from the honest business people who simply won't give the attention and service that I will. I am 100% positive that if they engage with me they are in the best hands possible. Call this unbridled hubris if you want but I call it confidence based on experience and mission.

I lead with their interest, pay close attention during the process and stay attached, following up regularly, long after the sale has been consummated, even when I have no further sale to make. I ask for problems so that I can address those issues before they have to call and alert me to them. I ensure that their experience with me is the easiest, most enjoyable, seamless sales experience they've ever had and that they feel great about the money they traded for my services.

I understand the difficulty in not feeling personally offended by the parade of "no"s, hang ups, closed doors and lost deals. I deal with it all the time and as I just said, I make sales intensely personal. In fact I know that is my edge but I employ yet another reframe to separate the rejection of the deal from the rejection of Frank.

It's Logically, Not Emotionally, Personal

While the business is always personal, it's not emotionally personal. It's not like in tenth grade when Mary Jane Miller turned me down for a movie date and I moped around for a week. It is logically personal. There is a difference.

I think about it and reframe it in a way that I feel bad for the client for making a poor choice. There is no way they will get the level of personal service and attention from anyone else that they would have gotten from me. Instead of focusing on losing the business, my reframe has me focused on their folly, their misguided choice.

A LOSS CAN TURN INTO A WIN

And, BTW, I still reach out after losing the sale.

I put them into a lost deal cadence in my CRM and continue to follow up with bits of information or an offer to help if I'm needed.

As Harvey MacKay said, and I paraphrase, "I want to be number two on a lot of people's list so that I will be in position if/when number one fades."

I honestly feel sorry for them that they've chosen someone who, at best, won't measure up to the level of service I bring and, at worst, has fooled them and is dishonest or unscrupulous. I feel badly that they didn't allow me to personalize the proposal to the point that they'd get to know me and understand what I offer. I choose to believe that they made a wrong choice because they assumed who I am was just another sales guy with just another offer, but didn't take the time to find out the real differences and now they've made a poor choice.

Truthfully, I still get a little angry when a misguided buyer just takes the lowest price without understanding that the lowest price may not be the best deal. There is zero doubt in my mind that I will service the client better than anyone who does what I do and therefore choosing someone else can only result in a lesser experience for that client. Case closed!

That is how I reframe rejection. I project the pain on them. It's not me who is hurt by their rejection, it's them.

The Ending ...

I asked Larry Weiss his final thoughts on advising salespeople. I asked, "If you could create a matrix situation, like in the movie, and hook up a connector to the back of your sales rep's head to download three vital pieces of information, what would they be?"

EXPERT TAKES

A deep desire to be the best, become a student of the game, and know what is current and relevant in your business and with your customers.

The age of the seller is over; we are now living in the age of the customer. You must understand how the dynamic has changed.

There are no more hammers, no hard pressure closers; that style is gone.

The most important thing is trust. If the client doesn't trust you, you will have a difficult time doing business with them. Credibility and knowledge about the business is very important and knowing about their business is important too!

You need to share examples of how you've helped similar businesses in the same vertical. This adds credibility and trust to your offering!

You try not to come off as "salesey" – their definition. Salesy is too slick, too pushy, not someone who is listening and sincere.

We all need to listen to the client. We know that. We need to understand what they're asking and, if what they want isn't the right solution, we have to be able to say so even if it means losing the business.

Most salespeople don't walk away. They make an adjustment and try to make the wrong solution fit because the customer asked for it, instead of sticking with what they know is right and walking away if they have to. In the end the client doesn't remember that you agreed with them on the solution they insisted on. They just say, "Why did you sell me this thing that isn't right?"

I asked Debbie a similar matrix question. I wondered what couple of vital bits of information she would upload into their brains.

EXPERT TAKES

The ability to envision a world where everyone is using the product they're selling.

The difference between enthusiasm and blasé. Enthusiasm is love and passion for who you are and what you want to be and for the improvement of the person you're talking to.

Get the client to be the hero of the story, not the victim. He is elevated with you, not sold by you. In any story the hero doesn't know he has a problem. Then he finds it and messes up. When you talk to people you make them the hero and you become the little angel that helped them on their journey. It's all about them; all about the client. The hero becomes the hero because of how you write the story.

When I produce an audio program, I ask people who buy it to listen to it a few times. The reason is that when you listen to a program and an idea strikes you, your mind begins to massage that idea with your way of thinking about it or your brain will start to apply that idea to a situation you currently have. When these thoughts occur, you lose the next couple of minutes of the audio program.

I feel similarly about reading a book, especially an instructional book like *B2B Is Really P2P*. There are ideas in here that will get you thinking about your own situations and you will imagine applying those ideas. You can read the next couple of pages while ruminating about a particular idea and although you are actually reading the words, they aren't absorbed. So, just like an audio program, I encourage a re-reading of this book or, at the very least, a re-reading of the sidebars and chunks in bold.

We've covered a lot of ground here. We've retooled the seemingly simple act of meeting someone and shaking hands (be open, heart to heart, make soft eye contact, smile, say hello, lean in a bit and hold that closeness for a beat, get their name and repeat it – Chapter 7) and learned a lot about how body position can help us to gain rapport and assess where we stand (pun intended) with someone (Chapter 8).

Calibrating expressions, breathing patterns, color changes, and eye cues is going to take some review and real-life practice (Chapter 11). Noticing things like shallow breathing and slight color changes *without* drifting out of the conversation is the goal.

Listening for vocal preferences, word choice, pace and tone will bring you a deeper understanding of people and understanding leads the way in forming deeper bonds (Chapters 9 and 10). Listening for, and knowing the difference between a view from the ground and a view from the air can save your relationship life, not to mention an important sale (Chapter 12). The recognition of these vastly different styles will help you show respect and further your rapport, when others, without this knowledge, routinely display impatience or resignation and unwittingly damage rapport.

Learning to use the right language with mismatchers will help to ease the frustrations you've encountered with this very strong personality type and allow you to move forward with these folks, where before you've been held in check with their contradictory language and postures. Recognizing a matcher will save you tons of time by asking more probing questions and leading them to a place where contradiction is welcomed and considered productive. Understanding matchers and digging in will allow you to, more often, act on real agreement rather than just appeasement (Chapter 10).

You can practice mirroring right now and see instant results and, of course, we can always, listen, listen, and listen some more to create deeper relationships and be instantly well thought of (Chapter 9).

You know how strongly I feel about personal responsibility (Part One). Remember the wave experiment (Chapter 4)? The one where I randomly waved at people in cars while jogging? I did it in many different states and even in different countries, but the results were always the same. When I waved and smiled at someone, they waved and smiled back; when I didn't, they didn't. I know we create our own weather (Chapter 3), I know we have the ability to make every tomorrow different from today, or the next moment different from this one, if we *decide*.

If you're with me on this journey in human communications, rapport, persuasion, *et al.*, then you agree that *you* are responsible for the results or your encounters. You agree that *you* possess the ability to douse the flames of highly charged words rather than meet them with an accelerant. *You* can calibrate, lead and pace. *You* can mirror, match and actively listen to build and ensure rapport. Let others, who are less aware of these choices, this power, blame the world for their bad encounters with phrases like, "He misunderstood me" and "She mistook what I meant" and "That wasn't what I intended." You know that *you* are responsible for the results of your encounters. And though you understand what an awesome and sometimes difficult posture that is, you still own it.

You are responsible for the results of your encounters.

*Che causa de sua male piange
lo stesso: Who causes his own
troubles cries over the same.*

Do you remember when I talked about Joe and me in the florist/ gift shop (Chapter 13)? Do you remember that while we both may have had a proclivity toward meeting folks and having conversations, essentially, we created an immersion lab for selling and developed our sales gene? We did this innocently and without a specific intention but what resulted was growth of our sales gene – like the cartoon animation of the Grinch's heart – it grew three times the size in a veritable instant.

I remind you of Joe and me because I know that you sometimes look at people with a bit of envy, wondering how they make it look so easy. I know that you sometimes think that they were born with abilities beyond yours. I tell the story of Joe and me to debunk that notion. This idea of nature over nurture in a selling environment is nonsense. That person you're looking at with envy isn't better than you, she's just *trained* better than you. It may have been intentional training, like reading great sales books, attending seminars or going to Dale Carnegie, or it may be that it was serendipitous, like the accidental learning lab Joe and I made of the florist/gift shop. But it wasn't a trait they were born with like brown eyes or long legs.

I have a friend who grew up poor, very poor. His grandfather used to let him tag along as he gathered old garments from thrift shops, cut them up to form 12 x 12 inch squares of cloth, and then sold stacks of them as rags to gas stations on the streets of Brooklyn. My friend was ten years old and, through this grandpa's rag business, was immersed in sales. He learned to hustle, cold call, present, negotiate and close. If you met him today you'd think he was "a natural" but the truth is that none of us emerge from the womb with number one salesperson status stamped on us. We learn, intentionally and unintentionally, and those lessons have brought us to where we are at this moment.

If you want to be the number one salesperson in your company and your grandfather did not take you corner to corner cold calling mechanics during your formative years, what should you do? Jump in with both feet right now! Read everything you can get your hands on. Listen to Ziglar, Hopkins, Thompson, and Wingit.[11] Go to Carnegie, Robbins, Sandler and Toastmasters.[12] Subscribe to YouTube channels with great content from folks like Darren Hardy and Tim Ferris.[13] Join LinkedIn and Facebook sales groups.

You may not have had the immersion training that makes the early bloomers appear to be born with it, but there is no shortage of information available to you to catch up quickly. You can improve dramatically from today to tomorrow and the tomorrows that follow, if you're willing to learn and practice. You can get a veritable Ph.D. in selling from these sources and so many more. Just decide and take action.

The last part of personal responsibility I need to address is to keep in mind a saying I learned from a friend in Alcoholics Anonymous; "Don't compare your insides to someone else's outsides." We do this *all the time*. There are a bunch of facets to this concept that I want to talk about with you.

At the very least, comparing *outsides to insides* translates, somewhat to the old adage that says, "You can't judge a book by its cover." But this great AA saying goes deeper. It reminds me that I am, indeed, judging a book by its cover and, worse, I am comparing the cover to my contents. Seeing the Kardashians and being the Kardashians are two entirely different things.

Comparing self to other is most often destructive for a few reasons. The insides to outsides thing is real. You see, you know what your insides look like. You know your insecurities and anxieties. You know your fears and foibles. But you don't know those things about another. You only know what you see on the outside, which is, maybe, 10% of the equation. Yet, your internal math calculates that they have it all going on and you suck. You compare *all* you know about you with *nothing* you know about them, and then you assume greatness for them and highlight only weakness for yourself. This is why inside to outside will never work. It's like comparing a pigeon to a peacock. Have you ever wondered why there were no carrier Peacocks?

I hope you bought in to win-win and will consider others first in negotiations (Chapter 19). Understanding what the other person wants and needs, displaying that understanding and are trying to accommodate those wants and needs will win you more contracts than bulling your way through with only your own objectives in mind. Negotiation is also about bringing value. Remember the lesson of my dad and the beer keg. "People don't pay for easy." When you make a concession of any sort, it is vital to establish the value of that concession first and please remember the phrase I have tried to drill in to the minds of thousands of sales people when you do offer a concession, "If I, will you."

Remember these two maxims:
"People don't pay for easy,"
and "If I, will you."

Be prudent with your time, and careful to whom you give it. Deliberately seek out people who move you up, rather than drag you down. Remember what the great Dr. Rob Gilbert, a college professor for almost 40 years says on this subject, "Show me the four or five people you hang around with. The average of their GPAs will be very close to your GPA."

In the end, I hope I have convinced you that selling is helping and that we are all selling all the time. Think about it for a moment. If I have convinced you, then my hypothesis is proven, and if I haven't, it isn't. After all, *B2B Is Really P2P* is all about strategies that convince so at the very core my job in writing it was to convince you!

We are all selling all the time.

I hope I have debunked some of the old sales stereotyping and helped you to see a few things in this area. The first is that we're all selling. Whether you're a teacher convincing students to read and study, a parent convincing a child to eat their spinach, a spouse convincing a spouse to modify a behavior, a coach convincing a player to give more, an usher convincing a rowdy patron to calm down, or any of the other hundreds of examples we can name of the everyday persuasions and negotiations we all are a part of, we are all selling. We all need strategies for greater rapport and to grease the wheels so they'll turn in our favor.

These techniques aren't only applicable to people who make a commission from convincing others because, the truth is, we all make a living convincing others to one degree or another.

The final point is that none of this works all of the time. There will be times that you lose the sales though you have applied everything you could think of to win it. There will be clients who leave and others you can't satisfy. You'll get turned down for the promotion and rejected by the cute guy at your yoga class. You'll fail with your kids and with your spouse. You'll feel frustration with your parents or your boss. You'll wrack your brain trying to find a way to get through to a coworker or employee. You'll suffer failure time and time again. It's okay. I won't be so gratuitous as to say something as trite as "All failure is only feedback" I won't disrespect the pain of rejection; this notion that "It isn't personal. They didn't reject you, they rejected your product." is a load of BS. Sales is fiercely personal. If you follow my philosophy then you understand and agree that they are rejecting you! *You* are what *you* are selling. *You* are the distinguishing factor that differentiates your offer from theirs. It sucks to lose. It sucks to be rejected.

> **You are what *you* are selling.
> You are the distinguishing
> factor that differentiates
> your offer from theirs.**

I want you to take away a newfound ability to debrief the communications knowledge you've learned here. Go back through a recent encounter, running it through the filters on these pages like matching, mismatching, air view, ground view, etc., and see what you might have done differently. In the end, you won't please everyone, and trying to is the surest way to fail.

Just like you select the friends you want to spend time with, you've got to select your clients too. Not everyone with interest in your product or service is your client. Not everyone can be pleased.

At the end of our interview, I asked Peter Chieco, "What is one thing you know now that you wish you knew then?" I want to share his answer with you.

EXPERT TAKES

Life is short don't hold back. Whatever dream you have, go for it now. Go for it with intensity.

I couldn't sleep on Sunday night waiting for Monday morning and I was in a business where you had to create your income.

You can't wait. You have to go get it!

Let me tell you one final story.

My dad and I take a trip to upstate NY every November for the opening of hunting season. It is a wonderful time, in a beautiful setting, with many of our cousins, uncles and extended family. It is much more about the camp and camaraderie than it is about the hunting, but I digress.

My dad was in his 70s and when I arrived to pick him up he was, of course, waiting at the door with his packed bag next to him and a cup of coffee for me. I grabbed the bag and brought it to my truck, came back to kiss my mom and grab the coffee, and off we went. The car ride up there is one of the best parts of the trip and we both look forward to those few hours in the car to talk one on one.

When we arrive at camp, Dad heads in with pastries and wine or a bottle of his homemade limoncello and I grab the bags. His is his old navy sea bag – a green canvas cylinder that's about 4 feet tall and maybe 18 inches wide. In order to get to anything in the bottom 6 inches of the bag, you first have to remove the 3½ feet of clothing on top. Get the picture? We are in a small cabin without much furniture and living out of our bags so you can imagine what a huge inconvenience this is for Dad (actually me, as he says, "Frankie, see if I packed my heavy socks" or "Cheech, go in my bag and see if you can get my long johns?").

On this particular trip I showed up with a new bag of my own. It was about 4 feet long and 2 feet wide. It laid flat, had a zipper opening the same size as the entire bag, 4 x 2, and allowed you to see all of the contents at once. It was on wheels and had a few outside zippered compartments for extra storage. In other words, it wasn't manufactured in 1950 for sailors to take onboard ship. My dad looked at that bag and said, "Wow, Frankie, that's a nice bag. I could use a bag like that. Look how I have to dig in mine to find anything. With this one, it's all right there in front of you."

Note to self: Buy Dad a bag like mine for Christmas.

When the weekend was over, I grabbed Dad's bag and mine (again he admired it) and threw them in the truck. We had a nice ride home, I brought Dad's gear into the house, had a coffee with my mom and hit the road. On the way, I called Deborah and said, "I know what to get Dad for Christmas."

Deborah bought and wrapped the bag and when Dad opened it he was really stoked. "I love this bag! It's just like yours with the big opening and the wheels and everything. Thank you so much!" He kissed Deborah and me and we basked in the moment of having given the perfect gift.

A few weeks later Dad called. "Frankie, I don't know about this bag."

"You don't know about it?" I prompted.

"I don't think it's for me."

"You don't?"

"No, I tried it out and it ain't quite right."

"What do you mean you tried it out?"

"I put a bunch of stuff in it and rolled it around the house a little and into the garage. I also tried to go up the stairs with it, but it just don't feel right. How much did you pay for it?"

"I don't know Dad. I think about $35.00"

"Okay," he said. "Just take it back and give me the money and I will find something else."

Now I know my dad as well as I know myself and I knew that he would show up next season with that same green canvas, navy sea bag. It wasn't so much about the bag as it was about change.

If this were a business transaction, I would not likely do well with it. My dad is not a suitable client for me. He is a long process kind of guy. He ruminates about things and constantly looks to make them better and to avoid a mistake. I know clients like my dad are out there and I know some of you are tuned in to this behavior and work well with clients like Dad; I do not and that's the point. Not everyone is your client.

A friend of mine, Steve, was bear hunting in Saskatchewan with an indigenous guide named Johnny Beavereye. Johnny was a throwback. He was literally of the land and the most spiritual man you'd want to meet. Johnny lived simply, and relied on the lake and the land for all of his nourishment and livelihood. Johnny was a man of few words, speaking only when necessary.

Steve saw a huge bear one morning but did not get a chance to harvest that animal. Back at camp he went on and on about a missed opportunity with that really big bear and Johnny simply said, "That is not your bear." My friend persisted, talking about the path the bear took and if he'd only walked a few yards this way or that he would have had an opening, that if only that pine tree wasn't there or the bear turned left instead of right. Johnny looked up and, again, said, "That is not your bear."

After the second time he said it, we understood what Johnny meant. In Johnny's spiritual world you are connected to the animals, birds and fish you harvest to eat and to clothe yourself. In Johnny's world there was a bear out there, connected to Steve, but this was not his bear and he needed to go and find the one that was.

That's the point with Dad and the bag too. Johnny would have said, "That is not your client." I'm not saying that you need to be spiritually connected to your client, but you do need to assess the fit. I see salespeople going at a sale like Sisyphus with the rock, constantly pushing but never getting to the top, never getting the deal. We know persistence is an essential quality to have in sales and in life. Quitting too soon is the downfall of a lot of otherwise talented people, however assessing a client and knowing when to move on is equally important.

If you've adopted some of the strategies I've outlined on prospecting, networking and referrals, you'll find your time is better spent on those activities than pursuing the wrong client. The trick here is threefold.

1. You've got to have enough other clients on your hot list so that you can release that client. Desperation makes us do stupid things.

2. You've got to believe in the processes I just outlined in Part Three so that you are certain your time prospecting will be more fruitful than chasing the wrong client.

3. You've got to recognize when a client isn't a fit.

There are a lot of tools in *B2B Is Really P2P* that you can put to use to improve your ability to gain rapport more quickly, spike sales, build great relationships and cement long-term loyalty but there are a few rules to the tools. Just like the tools in my garage, they only work well when they're well-oiled and charged up. Unfamiliarity with a tool, especially a powerful one, can cause great harm. Having the right tool within reach at the moment you need it is vital. How many times have you ruined a screwhead and created deeper issues because you didn't have the right screwdriver at the ready or, worse, had the right one in the garage but were too lazy or impatient to go and get it?

It's like that with the rapport tools in this book. You've got to be familiar with them to know when and how to use them so rereading, as I suggested earlier, is a must. Even if it's just highlighting some of the techniques to practice and rereading those occasionally. Practice is a must. You want to become unconsciously competent with rapport skills; you want to make them a natural part of the way you communicate. This takes time. It takes time in two ways. First it takes time to learn, practice and integrate these tools and, second, it takes time to use them. Communication is more about the sanding, shaping and finishing of a fine wood creation than it is about the initial chopping or sawing that initiates the process.

When I asked Larry Weiss to tell me about an epic failure he had and what he learned from it, his response was very interesting on a few different levels and underscored this idea of striving for unconscious competence.

EXPERT TAKES

[Long pause] I don't spend much time thinking about failures. However the one place I have to improve is that I have a lack of patience as it pertains to lazy people. And that doesn't even mean they are actually lazy. It's my definition of what is lazy and I have to watch what I do and what I say and my reactions, my face and body language with them. Sometimes I can be more brutal than I need to be. I need to work on that and I am conscious of it.

My goal is to help you to become a more trusted advisor, to be well liked and well thought of. My hope is to help you to create deeper, meaningful relationships with clients and friends and, indeed, to start to blur that line. My desire is that you learn this well and enjoy applying all you've learned so you can watch the world open up to you in a way it never has before.

It all begins with one decision – to be genuinely interested in other people. From there, from that sincere decision, listening becomes your natural posture.

Who Are the Experts?

Peter Chieco, CIMA®, grew up in the restaurant business, and learned early on the value of exceptional service. Entering the financial services industry in 1983, Peter dedicated himself to offering innovative solutions to complex wealth issues, along with the service that clients deserve.

A Managing Director at a major brokerage house, his is part of a top-notch team that advises on over $2 billion in assets. Their ability to identify, solve and serve specific client and family needs forms the cornerstone upon which their team was built.

In 2019, Peter was ranked once again as one of Barron's Top 1,200 Advisors and was recognized as one of *The Financial Times* Top 400 Financial Advisors. A frequent guest speaker and writer, his seasoned perspectives on investment strategies and markets have been featured by various media outlets throughout the United States.

Peter and his wife, Rose Ann, reside in Bedford Corners, NY. Peter's philanthropic efforts include a focus on health disorders, including the Cooley's Anemia Foundation, a not-for-profit charity helping children battle a fatal blood disorder. He currently serves as the National President for the Foundation, has testified before Congress and the FDA and is a frequent speaker about the disease.

He enjoys tending to his large organic garden and sharing food with his neighbors, friends and a local community center. He also enjoys traveling, fishing, hunting and spending time with his family.

The Interview

1. *Do you describe yourself as being in sales?*

Yes. Although I don't market myself as a salesman, I clearly say it to the people in my business, especially the rookies. We are salespeople. It's not a bad thing; it's a good thing. People have a bad perception of sales like a used car pushy guy doing whatever he needs to close. It's true that if I don't sell I don't survive; it's a fee for service business. But we aren't about selling to hit quota. We are about serving our clients' needs at a very high level and to do that we have to be good at selling.

2. *Talk about networking.*

I don't do a lot of networking. Taking care of my clients is how I grow the biz. When they do well, they refer us to their family and friends.

Once I fully appreciated that you only focus on your existing clients, and not actively push for referrals, the referrals started to flow in.

3. *Why do people choose to do business with you, personally?*

I have earned their trust. They know I have their best interest in mind and that I am going to work very hard and smart for their benefit. I never really dissected it. I am just the same way all the time to everyone, regardless of account size.

Always be ethical. We don't take short cuts. We don't work with wholesalers just because they take us to dinner or a ballgame. I always think, what is the benefit for the client? I am looking at the client not focused on my outcome, and that perspective if the key to our success.

4. *How did you learn to sell, to bring clients into your business?*

I grew up in the restaurant business and learned from Mom to treat people right and they will come back. Just that; treat people right. I watched my mom turn a complaint into a loyal customer by listening with respect and making sure she satisfied whatever they complained about.

I started out as a stock broker, aggressively pushing low-priced stocks at age 22.

I wanted to be a broker and no major firm would give me a chance. They said I was too young, too inexperienced. Then a waitress in the restaurant saw an ad for college grads – First Jersey was hiring.

They would pick one stock each month and you had to make 200 calls a day, 6 days a week. I learned about the power of my voice.

They would say we are selling this stock only and you keep selling until we say stop. I was calling out of my alumni directory to lawyers and accountants. They would pay us 10% of what we raised in principal. I saw young people making 40K monthly. I made $2,700 in my first month and thought that was fantastic. Then a friend at work told me we are ripping people off.

I was only there for two months; once I realized they were crooks, I left immediately. I learned that my voice was powerful and I could move people to action but I wanted to be ethical. So I went to another firm and my new manager told me to sell just as strong but sell conservative investments. I leaned to be careful with my voice.

I took years to find my groove. I lost people money at first but didn't lose the people. I think they knew that I was earnestly trying my best and were willing to accept a mistake and let me try again.

5. *What's the difference that makes the difference? What are three things you can name that separate you?*

My team and I are old school. No one will outwork us.

We live in a service model. Getting back to people right away and, additionally, anticipating what they will want to know and reaching out proactively.

I am very good at protecting families when there is a life event. Sometimes you have a strong leader who is heading the investment charge for the family and when he or she is gone, often, the remaining family members are at a loss of what to do. This is when we shine best, and the plan we created previously allows for peace of mind.

I also try to help guide the family leader to see a way for the family after he or she is gone so it is sustainable. We continually stay in touch with our clients, so we don't miss the opportunities to add value.

6. *What is one thing you know now that you wish you knew then?*

Life is short don't hold back. Whatever dream you have, go for it now. Go for it with intensity. I couldn't sleep on Sunday night waiting for Monday morning and I was in a business where you had to create your income. You can't wait. You have to go get it!

Frank Fusaro is a CPA who co-founded and serves as President of The Forum Group, a 100-person, Veteran-owned recruitment and consulting firm established in 1974. He developed a lecture series on Recruitment and Retention, which is presented to Big Four, National and Regional CPA firms and Corporations nationally. He served as Vice President and on the Executive Committee and Board of the NY State Society of CPAs. He served on the Advisory Board and was the principal fund raiser for the Society's Career Opportunities in Accounting Profession Program, which focuses on recruitment of minorities for the profession.

He is a recipient of three awards presented by the CPA Society, including "The Outstanding CPA in Industry Award," the "Arthur Dixon Award" for community service and the "Lifetime Achievement Award" presented by the H/R professionals of the member firms of the Society for contributions made to the Human Resources profession.

He is the past President and current Chairman of the Columbus Citizens Foundation, a 600-member, philanthropic organization. He serves on the Board of the Cooley's Anemia Foundation, St. Vincent's Services and the Tobin School of Business of St. Johns University. He developed an Adopt A Scholar Program for the Columbus Foundation, which has raised over twenty million dollars to date to provide scholarships for children of need as well as an annual event, which has raised over five million dollars to treat Thalassemia, a fatal children's blood disorder.

He received the title of Commendatore of the Legion of Merit by the President of Italy and was honored by the Cooley's Anemia Foundation, the Columbus Foundation and La Scuola di Italia for his charitable works. He received the Outstanding Alumni Medal from St. John's U. For 6 years he served as Chairman of the Annual "Columbus Day Parade" on Fifth Avenue and currently directs its worldwide telecast. He was a finalist in Ernst and Young's Entrepreneur of the Year Program.

The Interview

1. *Do you consider yourself a salesperson?*

Yes. A salesperson is not the first one with a lampshade on his head slapping backs at a party. A salesperson is someone who has intelligence, and a very distinct work ethic.

When I talk to young people about selling in this business, I say, "You know, when I was a kid, there was a comic strip, Joe Palooka. He was a very handsome, blond-haired, blue-eyed monster and they made this comic book character into a toy. He was there in his boxing trunks. He was three of four feet tall; basically a big upright balloon with a metal piece, like a ball or something in the bottom so you'd hit the toy and it would fall down backward and bounce right back up. Yeah, yeah, that's what a salesperson has to be. He has to be the guy who can take the punch and come back."

It's as simple as that. I mean, there are tools and approaches that you need to understand to be a good salesperson. But most of it's got to be what's inside of you. And that's what most people don't have. And that's why salespeople are so coveted because they have that thing inside them that keeps going and they are the people that make the business run. Without sales you have nothing.

You could have the best product in the world, the best price but if you don't know how to sell it it's not going anywhere and, conversely, a good salesperson could sell a mediocre product.

2. *Think about business owners that are selling. Do you think people take to it naturally, do you think they shy away from it, do you think they force themselves, or what?*

I think a sales aptitude is very important in a business owner however, it's not critical. If the business owner is smart enough to develop the right product and hire good salespeople and, you know, give them good direction or hires that sales manager that can run them. You could hire skills you don't personally have. You don't have to have every skill in the world to be a business owner, right? But you certainly have to have people that can go out and bring business in. Selling is the one thing all business owners need to do whether they do it themselves or hire.

3. *What do you think is the best way to find new clients? If you're advising a new business owner or a new salesperson, what do you tell them?*

You do your homework. You do your due diligence, you create a roster of targets. And it's got to be an endless roster, because it's going to be one after the other after the other. And then you try to get your foot in the door and get their attention in some way. You try to understand what their requirements might be.

I told you, I was selling car radios and stereos and didn't really know what the hell I was doing. So I sold Kmart by going out and going to a couple of stores and looking at their products and seeing what they were selling to find comparable radios that we had in stock. Then I went to the buyer and said, "Okay, I don't know what you're paying for these radios, but this is how mine compare to what you're selling. Here are the specifications, and so on, mine is better and at the price I'm willing to give you, you will enjoy an 80% markup. I mean, I have no way of knowing what you're paying. But I know that I don't think that you're operating on an 80% margin."

So the point of that is really that you did your homework and you found the best way to get their attention.

Yes. You have to sell differentiators.

4. *Tell me about finding business because you brought in a ton of business, right?*

Yeah, but I was a young CPA and I pulled out all the CPA firms and I sat with that list and, you know, again, a few minutes at a time I would pursue them. I would be persistent about getting in front of them.

And I also was very active in the New York State society of CPAs. The New York State society was run by mostly the small to medium firms, the big firms don't have an interest. So I met all the principles of the small to medium sized firms mostly, and they got to know me a little bit. And, you know, they allowed me to call on them. So, essentially, I went to where they played. Then I made sure to sit on a committee. And you know, when you get involved in nonprofits, associations, trade associations, charities, nobody wants to do anything. So if you stick your hand up and say, "I'll do it; I'll volunteer," you become the kingpin.

After a phone call with a young man who is a salaried recruiter for a hospital system but is considering coming to Forum, Frank said:

Okay. So what do I do with that? Because that's a kid that's got three years in recruiting and reached out to me because I have a need in my HR placement world. But see, this kid, he doesn't want to be a salesman. He doesn't want to, you know, be under a quota or whatever so I try to appeal to someone like that and explain that my people are top line producers and very valuable to me.

I feel like saying, "You're missing the boat; they don't care about you. They're about the medicine. They're about the patients. They're about revenue generation, right? They're not about HR."

He says, "I enjoy servicing that area and being a business partner."

That's nonsense. He's basically a caddy. He's servicing the golfer.

You go to the golfer and say, "What do you need? Okay, I'll try and find it. Right?" Conversely, if he came here, and he'd go out and recruit a guy for a hundred grand, he'd get a nice commission. Over there he gets an "Attaboy" from the company. When he finds someone for double or triple that salary, which isn't uncommon, he'd generate a five figure commission for himself.

So what do you want? A five figure commission or an attaboy?

5. *What makes you good at bringing in business? What is it about you specifically?*

It starts with the basics of opening the door, getting in front of a person and learning how to relate to them. You walk into an office, okay, you look around, right? The guy's a golfer, the guy went to St John's, the guy did this or the guy did that that, the guy's got six kids or whatever. Today, you do a LinkedIn search before you even get there. I never go visit the person without looking at LinkedIn first and finding out something about them, where they went to school, where they grew up, what company they started at, etc.

You start out with them being impressed that you spent time learning about them and the company. You find the common ground to begin to relate to a person and continue to ask questions, learning to understand their needs and requirements so you can fulfill them. You don't go and call on somebody in a bank without looking them up and the bank first.

I interviewed a guy for five minutes this morning he said, "How many people do you have?" I said about a hundred or something like that. He said, "Oh what areas are you in?"

What the hell? You're seeing me about a job in my company and you don't look at the website? You don't know the areas that we work in? You don't know anything about us? You didn't even spend five minutes on our website?

6. *I want to get back to something you said about having a strong work ethic and understanding people's needs. I know you want somebody that shows up and wants to work but what other essential ingredients do you think you have to have to be successful?*

I've said this a million times, lots of people are born with the brains to be successful but only a handful of people have the heart to be successful. You have to have the heart to be a salesperson. You have to be focused, you have to be willing to take the punches.

This guy at the hospital, he's got an inbox and outbox okay? He arrives in the morning and they say we need a nurse practitioner, we need this person, we need that person. He goes and advertises and he finds some candidates. He does things to get your job filled because that's his job – to get stuff in the inbox to the outbox. All he wants to do is get some resumes and give it to the guy who needs the position and then he's out; he's a middleman.

He tells them, "You want to see Dr. so and so on Tuesday at 11 and then at 5 o'clock or 5:30 he goes home. He gets his paycheck and as long as he's performing for the hospital and they need him, he gets that paycheck and at the end of the year he gets a 3% raise. He takes his couple of sick days here and there, spends two weeks at the Jersey Shore, he's got a little house, he's happy, nothing wrong with that.

But my people, salespeople, they can't be that way. They have to have the heart to come in, call the clients, call the candidates, go back and forth and back and forth trying to get things done.

You know I tell people this business is not like being a professional golfer. You're on the 72nd hole of the tournament and if you make the putt you're in first place and win a million bucks, but if you miss the putt you're in second place you get $750,000. In this business if you miss the putt you get nothing. You have to be able to deal with that; you have to be able to deal with getting an email on Sunday night after you did a big deal with the guy who is supposed to start on Monday and he says, "I'm very sorry but I never thought this was going to happen. They made me a counter offer. This thing came out of the blue. My sister is in Delaware and I have to take care of her, I fell in the shower blah, blah, blah."

That happens all the time and you have to come in and write a drop out after you already have that money counted. You have to have some resilience to deal with that.

7. *So, you think that resilience is the number one thing besides, obviously, work ethic, desire?*

Intelligence matters too. It's not rocket science to sit down with a kid and say, before you go call on Joe Blow, find out what they do and learn something about him and the potential of the account. We try to say that The Forum Group is a veteran-owned business. We've been around for 45 years and we have a great reputation. We can help you in the area that we're going to talk about but isn't it nice that when you call me I have the ability and technology to look at the entire enterprise with all the other things that we do. So you don't just walk in and say I'm The Forum Group. Give me the job because they say there are two million staffing firms out there. Why should I do business with you?

8. *I know how you grew up so I understand fear of failure and your intense desire. Plus, I think the military service has a little bit to do with it. I think it helped to train us in ways of discipline that other people don't have. My question is, can you teach this*

to somebody? If I give you anybody of reasonable intelligence
can you teach them this or do they have to have it in their belly?

Look, you could make a five into a seven, okay? You can manage your five to a seven or mismanage a five down to a two or
three for that matter, but you can't make a five into a nine.

Training and teaching is critical. However, they can only
take you so far. It's the execution that's the trick. I have to go
out and recruit a seven for my business. That doesn't mean he's
got to be the brightest burning church candle, okay. He's got to
have that desire, desire, desire, desire! He's got to look around
at people who are successful here and say I want that, that he
is motivated.

I'm involved with a few different charities. You know me
from Cooley's anemia. I was never touched by Cooley's anemia
personally. Nobody in my family was ever affected by Cooley's
but when they put that baby in my arms I got a little bit choked
up and that was that. I was done. You know it's not a lot for me;
I probably do $10,000 a year for Cooley's but I bring support
from the Columbus Club and I've been involved for 25 to 30
years but it never stops. You gave your word and you're good for
it until the end, until the kids are healthy.

Glad we got to talk today. I'm not even supposed to be
here. I go back to Florida usually on Thursday nights but I'm not
going tomorrow night because the airfare is $500 because this
Presidents' week. I fly in the back of the plane every week for
$105 bucks, now I'm going to give them $500 for the same seat?
Not me.

I have guys that owe me $50,000 or $100,000. That doesn't
bother me. There are some things that are just ingrained in
you from childhood. Somebody said to me "You know you can
afford it?" Sure, but I'm not going to pay United Airlines $500
for a seat that cost me $100 the week before. It doesn't make
sense. It's just in my nature; who I am.

Debbie Kosta, Personal Results Specialist, has worked alongside Tony Robbins, promoting his life changing events on a global scale. She is inspired by Tony's mission to transform lives, and has made it her life's purpose to help people achieve the life they desire.

She holds a BA in English Literature, and is currently pursuing a Master of Wine distinction. As a top producer on Tony's live events sales team, she is motivated by human potential. She is also an active contributor for Operation Underground Railroad, and is committed to help stop human trafficking.

Debbie is a New Yorker, born and bred, and enjoys her time with the people and things she loves most: her kids, writing her book, traveling, biking, great friendships and tasting and reviewing wine.

The Interview

1. *How did you start?*

I studied writing. I hated salespeople or at least I hated to be sold to. I thought they were fake! I went to Cypress and some people approached me and offered me a job with Robbins because I could speak English.

I went there and saw Tony's poster and then I heard salespeople talking to clients and talking to them like they were friends. They gave encouragement, and advice like they were friends. And this is what I do in my life anyway. I love people. So, I gave it a try.

They were all experienced people and I wasn't, and I was intimidated. I loved speaking to people about what they want in life and how they can do it. I studied Tony's tools and saw this was the missing piece. I had a good instinct about people – when to call and when to leave things alone. I am a very good listener. Put the phone on mute if you have to but listen to what they are saying and not saying.

2. *How important is networking?*

The hardest working person in the company is Tony. He is out there doing everything – raising money and giving money. He is always out there. He has a great presence on SM [social media] too. Leads come in because of his networking. We did a little advertising but mostly getting the word out. Being an ambassador for the product is the best sales tool. I am building an outstanding life which is what I am selling.

It's go, go, go! But grounded and spiritual. You have to walk your talk. Especially with personal development. You have to ask difficult questions.

You have to build rapport. It's not just talking about the weather; I have to earn the right to probe. I am a risk taker and a little audacious. I ask great questions because of the way I ask. Some people want a gentler approach so I have to listen for that.

My *rule* is that I listen to know how to ask and to see if they are ready for a hard question. I have become trained to listen. I respect them, their time, their past and future. I give value before I ask the tough questions. It may be advice, it may be a suggestion, but I add value and get an "Oh, wow! She helped me."

I give some of the advice that I learned from Vaynerchuk, Robbins, Rohn, Dyer, etc.

Gary's book, *Jab, Jab, Jab, Right Hook,* is value, value, value, sale.

This is what Tony does. He always gives value. This is how I ask the sensitive questions.

There have been times that I didn't listen well and asked a question that was too strong and blew it.

It takes a lot of practice for many, many years to listen well and earn the right to ask the tough questions.

I want to uncover the six human needs. I say "This is a huge step"… and I pause. I use the pause almost as a question. It prompts them to answer deeply.

3. *Why do people choose to do business with you, personally?*

I have a great team of salespeople here. I think that what sets me apart is I respect people and love what I do. Not that they don't; it's just more obvious with me. I come from an honest place. I want to be part of the solution and my sincerity comes through.

I really want to help change the human condition and my business can do that. I am 75–80% referrals; I don't even get leads from the 800 number.

I always ask who do you know who can benefit from this learning the way you did? Who do you know that you'd like to add some sunshine into their lives?

4. *How did you learn to sell; to bring clients into your business?*

I thought I would get some training, but it was like, "Here are your leads, call them." I was a calling machine, fumbled and learned. I was embarrassed, and I didn't know how to ask for the business. Then, suddenly, it came to me. I thought they will benefit from this, and of course you have to pay for something you will benefit from. I did get some training; he helped me with the filling out of forms – the work part – but the people part I just came to on my own. We learned a lot by listening to Tony and absorbing his philosophy. As a literature major I had read a lot. I'd hear Tony say something and think I heard a form of it from Aristotle or Plato. Tony knows how to say things so people will understand. Tony is relevant to today. He is always learning.

5. *What's the difference that makes the difference? What are three things you can name that separate you?*

I don't hear no. I don't hear objections. I say a prayer that God will help me to help people. I believe in what I do. I can't let go of someone who I believe needs this. That's why I don't hear no. I envision them in the room. I envision them having the life they've shared that they want with me and I don't hear no; I hear not yet. So I don't let them go.

Second is that I don't chase after the money. A lot of people work triple what I work because they are focused on the wrong thing. I focus on the person and the money follows.

Three is asking the right questions. I do keep an eye on revenue but number one for me is the person in front of me. I plant ideas. So first it's that person but then I say, "Let's get your whole company on board."

I got a guy and made him come one day for a low price. I didn't even know if I was allowed to do that. I just told him $100 for one day of a four-day program. I paid it because I thought he would spread it to maybe 100 other people. He ended up buying 6,000 tickets from me. He was the son of a successful corporate person and he used his dad's money to promote the underdogs. It was a cause for me too so number four is that I bring groups.

I use my time wisely. I come from a place of abundance. I believe it's out there for me. Coming from abundance gives you an air of confidence; it gives that person you're talking to the confidence. (It's a lion and mouse thing.) They say, "How do you get those big deals, Debbie?" I don't get leads, I am happy to teach you. They call me and what do they ask? What are some of the tricks you do on sales force? They think my secret sauce is wizardry of sales force or some magic manipulation. They don't realize or want to realize that I ask the right questions. That I probe deeper. That I begin by wanting to help.

How you do one thing is how you do anything. This shows up in their lives where they don't go for the gold in life; they're satisfied with mediocre. I'm not. You have to have a big enough why, right?

My personal why is my kids' private school, college, travel, whatever. If you just want to make enough – and by the way I hate that word "enough" – maybe you should have a much bigger why.

I trained a girl. She managed to go from the bottom to above average, and then she plateaued. She said, "I make enough now."

I said, "Don't you want to live better? Maybe to go to Italy?" She is stagnated. If you're not growing, you're dying. Stagnation at forty something is going down; not staying even.

My place is of growth and contribution in this world.

6. What is one thing you know now that you wish you knew then?

I wish I knew back then that people are always looking for solutions. When they're not, they don't like it. Back then I was interrupting them when I cold called. Now I feel like I'm doing them a favor by calling them because even if they don't know they're looking for solutions, they are, and I remind them.

7. What's the best advice you can give to a new salesperson on their first day on the job?

Believe in themselves and become best friends with the product because without passion there is nothing. Sales used to be a bad word. I love sales.

8. If you could do a matrix, like in the movie, and hook up a connector to the back of your sales rep's head to download three vital pieces of information, what would they be?

Ability to envision a world where everyone is using the product they're selling.

The difference between enthusiasm and blasé. Enthusiasm is love and passion for who you are and what you want to be and for the improvement of the person you're talking to.

Get the client to be the hero of the story not the victim. He is elevated with you; not sold by you. In any story the hero doesn't know he has a problem. Then he finds it and messes up.

When you talk to people you make them the hero and you become the little angel that helped them on their journey. It's all about them; all about the client. The hero becomes the hero because of how you write the story.

9. *Are great sales people born or made?*

Made. We are all born with heart and mind and when the heart and mind get inspired by the product and the process and you get passionate about it, you become a great salesperson.

You have to have passion. I thought I was a writer all my life. When my mom said, "You're bad with numbers. You will never be a business person," I believed it because, you know, writers, artists are supposed to be bad with numbers and business. Then I went to Tony and learned I could handle numbers well; I could be a strong business person. You can't accept limiting beliefs.

Wayne Dyer was dropped off at an orphanage at six years old. The other kids were all crying and complaining. He reframed it into an opportunity to become self-reliant.

Larry Weiss, the President and Chief Executive Officer of Atlantic-Tomorrows Office, has forged a professional resume defined by a sense of hard work, ambition and the desire to continually improve his business and customer service. He has achieved a great level of success and has distinguished himself among business executives through an unceasing eagerness to create a "working model" of collaboration and intelligent productivity.

For more than 44 years, he has developed a unique acumen within the copier and office products industry, and today is noted as one of the foremost entrepreneurs in his field. Upon graduating from Hofstra University in 1973 and quickly thereafter beginning his career with Xerox, Mr. Weiss soon began to garner the expertise that would serve him exceedingly well in the coming years.

In 1982, Mr. Weiss "rescued" Atlantic Photocopy from bankruptcy, and as the adage attests, "the rest is history." A small, struggling operation, which had a staff of 5, has today become an ever-growing business, employing 500 trained men and women and boasting a clientele of more than 20,000. The time-honored, "customer-first" and altruistic approach to business has served Atlantic's CEO very well throughout his career, and the forward-thinking mindset espoused at today's Atlantic continues to set the tone for a high standard of excellence.

Today, Atlantic's business "evolution" has brought it from a leading copier company to a progressive, state-of-the-art and technologically-superior organization that is capable of providing a multi-faceted approach to a wide array of professional services. It is that fully comprehensive approach to office management that gives true meaning to "tomorrow's office." From IT-managed services to network solutions, backup and disaster recovery, professional technology, security services, managed print services and more, Atlantic has become a nationwide industry leader.

From his earliest days as an aspiring entrepreneur, Mr. Weiss has maintained a passion for working with executives and executive management teams, providing invaluable assistance to others toward the development of effective and efficient strategies as well as "best practice" approaches to improve their professional and personal lives. Spanning more than four decades, he has taken a genuine interest in the well-being and happiness of his colleagues and employees, and through skills honed over the years, he has helped so many realize their true potential.

Toward that same end, Mr. Weiss has continually insured that a spirit of philanthropy remains a driving force of Atlantic, and with a sincerely-placed effort to "give back" to the community, his company maintains an annual budget of more than $1 million specifically dedicated to not-for-profit organizations.

In addition to his many professional accomplishments, Mr. Weiss has selflessly donated his time and efforts to many worthy organizations throughout the years. He is a board member of the National Kidney Foundation and St. Christopher's Inc., as well as an enthusiastic supporter of the Jillian Fund, New Jersey's Englewood Hospital, the Fresh Air Fund, Cooley's Anemia Foundation and the New Jewish Home. Mr. Weiss was an integral member of the JCC Board of Directors for 16 years, and continues to contribute in an honorary role. Additionally, he formerly served on the board of directors for the Hudson Valley Make-A-Wish Foundation. His tireless work with the JCC Maccabi baseball team for many years is a testament to his passion for youth sports.

Mr. Weiss remains quite proud of Atlantic's accomplishments and the company's standing within the business community. No achievement in his professional life, however, can equal the sense of pride and passion Mr. Weiss holds for his amazing family. Linda, his loving wife of 45 years, is continually rapt in her own philanthropic endeavors, and in tandem with Mr. Weiss and an indefatigable spirit has been instrumental in bringing positive change to so many lives. The couple's two sons, Jason and Adam, have established themselves as integral parts of Atlantic's success. Jason serves as the company's General Legal Counsel and lives in New York City with his wife, Nicoll, and Atlantic's newest "executive," their son Jayden. Adam serves dual executive roles as General Manager and Vice President of Sales at Atlantic, and along with his wife, Taryn, also resides in NYC.

As Mr. Weiss continues to expand the Atlantic horizons, he does so with a very grateful and self-effacing perspective. Thankful for those who have helped facilitate his successful journey thus far, and aspirational about the business opportunities that lie ahead.

The Interview

1. *How did you start?*

I started bartending while going to college. I loved it. I loved the cash I was making in nightly tips but felt like that lifestyle was incompatible with my goals of getting married and having a family one day. I saw an article about Xerox and their sales reps driving expensive cars, like Porsche, Corvette and BMW, and said, "That's for me."

I went after it. I had four interviews at four different branches and got a job as a sales rep. I was good at it. I got this! It seemed to come naturally, like being instantly good at a sport.

I had been selling my whole life. My homeroom was also the home economics room, so I sold the pizza and the cookies the home economics students baked.

In my first year at Xerox I was the number one sales rep out of 80 in the branch. I realized quickly that sales is a profession, while most people think of sales differently. There is a low barrier of entry for a sales position. It's not like you need a lot of schooling or a specialized degree to get in, but I look at sales as a profession not unlike being a doctor or a lawyer. I think it requires as much education as a doctor or a lawyer though maybe of a different kind.

2. When did you consider yourself a success?

I was fair at everything but never really great at anything so I always felt I was successful. Good enough was good enough. Then I found selling.

After my first year at Xerox I felt like a real success. I made $21,432 in 1974 when the average household income was about $10,000. (It was actually $13,093 according to multpl.com.) I was on top of the world!

Then the next year I made $36,000. I wall papered my mother's wall with $100 bills. The average income was still about the same. I knew I had hit my stride. I knew I loved sales and copiers. The success pushed me to learn more and more about sales and leadership and I'm still a student of the game. Sales and leadership became my passion and still are today!

3. Take me through a typical Larry Weiss morning.

Up early and in the office 5:15–5:30 AM; review emails in detail. Review all of the information and assignments for the day, week, and month. I have a morning meeting with one of my direct reports at 7:30 AM almost every morning.

Now it's around 9:00 AM and the meetings for the day begin. I still go out on sales calls some days; that's in the mix.

4. How different is that morning from a Larry Weiss morning in 1974?

I got up a little later then but I was still in earlier than anyone else, 7:30 AM or so, reviewing the day, preparing for appointments. The day ended around 4:30 PM when I went to the gym.

5. Do you have mentors or role models and how did they help you?

I've had many different people throughout my selling career and have learned from all. As far as a true mentor, my first trainer was not responsible to train me but he took me under his wing. He was a territory rep at Xerox, not a manager. I am still in touch with him.

I have a business coach and have worked with her for over 20 years and she is also my mentor.

6. What's the difference that makes the difference? What are three things you can name that separate you?

You must be relevant! Presenting valuable resources and information to your clients. Example: Around 1984, I looked at what else to do and took on mailing equipment. We grew to one of the top three mailing equipment dealerships in the country and then sold that business.

In the late 90s, as copiers were becoming part of the network, we were asked to do connect work – IT. So we went in that direction and built IT services. That division delivers revenue as midsize copier companies do today.

7. What drives you to keep achieving more?

The excitement of the challenge! We have close to 500 employees.

We just had awards night and despite the fact that we have a large territory and some people have to drive over four hours, most employees attend the event (80% turnout). I love looking at the faces of the recipients when they get awards and seeing how they have grown to become leaders at Atlantic. That really gets my juices flowing.

Making Atlantic the best company to work at and providing a client with the best and latest technology, to operate more efficiently than the competition.

8. What was your greatest failure and what did it teach you?

[Long pause] I don't spend much time thinking about failures. However the one place I have to improve is that I have a lack of patience as it pertains to lazy people. And that doesn't even mean they are actually lazy. It's my definition of what is lazy and I have to watch what I do and what I say and my reactions, my face and body language, with them. Sometimes I can be more brutal than I need to be. I need to work on that and I am conscious of it.

9. Growing a business requires trade-offs. What is non-negotiable for you?

The trade-off is family and friends. You must figure how not to miss some of the events while your children are growing up or you may regret this later or, worse, they may never forgive you.

The "Cat's in the Cradle" song by Harry Chapin was always in my head. I did the best; hopefully my wife and boys feel the same.

Non-Negotiable —

- Poor work ethics
- Not achieving quota
- Laziness
- Poor attitude
- Lack of effort

10. What's the best advice you've given to a rep on their first day on the job?

The business is not what you think it is. This is not a nine to five business. You have to constantly be looking for business. You have to practice and learn. Selling is a profession you have to practice. You create the number of opportunities and the more opportunities you create the better you will do.

Malcolm Gladwell has the 10,000 hour rule. 10,000 hours of deliberate practice will make you world class at anything. When I started I knocked on 100 doors a day. That's like the 10,000 hours. That will make you great but nobody listens. Nobody knocks on 100 doors a day anymore, or even makes 100 quality phones calls!

11. Pretend I'm a salesperson who missed quota three months in a row. What would you say to me?

We have a do or die policy that lays out activity goals and revenue goals. We clearly understand that you may not hit your revenue quota in the first few months. There are a lot of factors at play to bring in business in the first couple of months but activity is within your control. Doing the activities is a choice. If you choose not to do it; you made that choice. So we look at both the revenue target and the activity targets. After those first 90 days you need to be at least 100% in one or the other or the policy says you're gone.

12. Who is the best salesperson you know and what makes them the best?

Chabad Rabbis. Rabbi Perl (Mineola). They raise lots of money. They are trained professionals who make you feel good about yourself. They provide you with what you need. My wife is Italian. The Rabbi makes her feel like the best Jewish woman on the planet.

13. What do you think motivates salespeople the most?

No one can motivate anyone. We can energize and assist but you have to motivate yourself. What motivates successful salespeople is desire to be the best. They want recognition; they want to walk into the stadium as the clean-up hitter.

14. If you could do a matrix, like in the movie, and hook up a connector to the back of your sales rep's head to download three vital pieces of information, what would they be?

A deep desire to be the best; become a student of the game and know what is current and relevant in your business and with your customers.

The age of the customer is over; we are now living in the

age of the seller. You must understand how the dynamic has changed.

There are no more hammers, no hard pressure closers; that style is gone.

The most important thing is trust. If the client doesn't trust you, you will have a difficult time doing business with them. Credibility and knowledge about the business is very important and knowing about their business is important too!

You need to share examples of how you've helped similar businesses in the same vertical. This adds credibility and trust to your offering!

You try not to come off as "salesey" which is their definition. Salesy is too slick, too pushy, not someone who is listening and sincere.

We all need to listen to the client. We know that. We need to understand what they're asking and if what they want isn't the right solution, we have to be able to say so, even if it means losing the business.

Most salespeople don't walk away. They make an adjustment and try to fit the wrong solution in because the customer asked for it, instead of sticking with what they know is right and walking away if they have to. In the end the client doesn't remember that you agreed with them on the solution they insisted on, they just say why did you sell me this thing that isn't right?

When I feel comfortable buying it is clearly when they understand what I'm asking for. They're not baiting and switching and trying to get me to buy what they want to sell. They understand what I want.

People don't buy from the best, they buy from the less risky! You know the old saying "No one ever got fired for buying IBM or Xerox." Being less risky is about being trustworthy and having credibility. Here is our seal of satisfaction that mitigates the risk. Or here is how we stand behind our offer so you can feel safe. (It's your insurance policy.)

Proof that you will do what you say makes it less risky. Not everyone is analytical and knows all of the details to the level that there is no risk; most people make emotional buying decisions so taking away risk is a big factor.

15. *Why do some people excel while others flounder?*

It's like I said before, they have a deep desire to be the best. Come in on any given morning and you will see some people pounding out the work while others are still talking about the Yankee game from last night. The high achievers in sales set high goals for themselves, are students of the game and love to win!

A lot of people set goals but don't do anything differently to achieve them. The three big lies people tell are: I want to lose weight, I want to stop smoking, and I want to make more money. They're lies because they say it but don't act on it. If they were really serious, they would just do it! Not wait for New Year's Eve to make false promises to themselves.

16. *Who is the smartest person you know?*

I am very fortunate to know quite a few very smart people. However if I have to pick one it would be Ace Greenberg, CEO of Bear Sterns. May he rest in peace!

17. *Think back to your initial selling days. What did you like/ dislike about the sales process?*

Selling is a game! I love this game more than I love baseball. If there was a part of the game I dislike, it is when I don't win! [LOL!]

18. *What keeps you up at night?*

Nothing!

19. *What is one thing you know now that you wish you knew then?*

The importance of patience! I don't jump to solutions as fast. I will listen, ask questions and then make a decision.

20. *What does your success mean to you and what are your goals now?*

Success means helping others achieve their goals and making a difference in the community! My goals today are to continue to grow the business, so that I may have the resources to make a positive impact on the communities that we serve.

21. *What's your favorite TV show? Book? Movie?*

TV Show: Curb Your Enthusiasm
Book: *Outliers* by Malcolm Gladwell
Movie: *The Pursuit of Happyness*

End Notes

Selling to the Sopranos

[1] Uptime, in Neuro-Linguistic Programming (NLP) terms, means complete engagement. It means total focus on the listener. Uptime means you are zoned in and active. You are managing your eye movements to convey understanding, warmth, surprise or concern. You're leaning in, smiling or frowning with the speaker. You are verbally showing your attention with words of affirmation or non-word sounds or a light touch, where appropriate, to assure the speaker you are in the conversation totally and to the exclusion of all else.

Chapter 5: Learning to Communicate Better

[2] Richard Bandler and John Grinder created neuro-linguistic programming, an approach to communication, personal development, and psychotherapy, in California in the 1970s. They claim there is a connection between neurological processes (*neuro-*), language (*linguistic*) and behavioral patterns learned through experience (*programming*), and that these can be changed to achieve specific goals in life. Bandler and Grinder also claim that NLP methodology can "model" the skills of exceptional people, allowing anyone to acquire those skills.

Chapter 8: Watch Those Feet!

[3] Selective attention is the idea that when you learn of or give your focus to something new, that new thing will seem to appear everywhere you are. Remember in Chapter 1 when I spoke about Mark the accountant and selective attention? I said if you decide to buy a blue Subaru because all you see around you are green Subarus and you want to be different, the

moment you decide the world will bring a virtual parade of blue Subarus to you. Selective attention is the term for this change in your awareness. We'll see selective attention again in Chapter 17 when discussing referrals.

Chapter 10: Behavioral Tools

[4]There are four types of communicators in the NLP system: Kinesthetic, Auditory, Reflective and Visual. Most people are a combination with one style being more dominant than the others.

Chapter 11: Calibration

[5]Martin M Broadwell, "Teaching for Learning," *The Gospel Guardian*, February 20, 1969.

[6]Alfred Korzybski, *Science and Sanity: An Introduction to Non-Aristotelian Systems and General Semantics* (1933).

Chapter 16: Networking

[7]The Junto, also known as the Leather Apron Club, was a club for mutual improvement established in 1727 by Benjamin Franklin in Philadelphia. The Leather Apron Club's purpose was to debate questions of morals, politics and natural philosophy, and to exchange knowledge of business affairs.

Chapter 17: Referrals

[8]Martin P. Seligman, *Authentic Happiness: Using the New Positive Psychology to Realize Your Potential for Lasting Fulfillment* (NY: Simon & Schuster, Inc., 2002).

Chapter 19: Negotiating

[9]Roger Fisher and William Ury, *Getting to Yes: Negotiating Agreement Without Giving In* (NY: Penguin Books, 1981).

[10]Stephen R. Covey, *The 7 Habits of Highly Effective People: Powerful Lessons in Personal Change* (NY: Simon & Schuster, 1989).

The Ending ...

[11] All these people specialize in speaking about business, sales and personal development.

[12] These names may look familiar because they are world-renown experts on building rapport. Toastmasters will help you to get comfortable speaking – to groups and to individuals.

[13] They'll inspire you to live your best life.

GET MORE INSPIRING ADVICE FROM FRANK

Do you want to build great relationships and cement long-term loyalty?

To book Frank to speak at your next event or get some one-on-one coaching, please call (732) 822-5990 or email frank@franksomma.com.

www.franksomma.com

www.twitter.com/fsomma

www.linkedin.com/in/frank-somma-473ab612

www.facebook.com/sommafrank

Made in the USA
Monee, IL
18 November 2020